Agapé

Unveiling the Darkness and Setting the

Captives Free

Freedom Series: Volume Two

F. Dean Hackett, Ph.D.

SPIRIT LIFE MINISTRIES INTERNATIONAL

pirit Life Ministries International

Discovering True Identity
Copyright © 2002 by F. Dean Hakcett, Ph.D.

This title is also available as an ebook. Visit
www.fdeanhackett.com/store

Requests for information should be addressed to Spirit

Life Ministries Publications, Hermiston, Oregon 97838

ISBN: 978-0615933658

All rights reserved. No portion of this publication may be
reproduced in a retrieval system, or transmitted in any
form or by any means – electronic, mechanical,
photocopy, recording, or otherwise – without the express
prior permission of Spirit Life Ministries Publications,
with the exception of brief excerpts in magazine articles
and/or other reviews.

Cover design: Stephanie Eidson
Cover photography: Pixabay
Interior Design: Rosilind Jukić

Originally published under the title: Mission Agape
Printed in the United States of America

I gratefully dedicate this work to my wife, best friend, mother of our children, and ministry partner for forty-three years.

Wanda, I love you and greatly admire you.

My Dear Wormwood,

I wonder you should ask me whether it is essential to keep the patient in ignorance of your own existence. That question, at least for the present phase of the struggle, has been answered for us by the High Command. Our policy for the moment, is to conceal ourselves...I do not think you will have much difficulty in keeping the patient in the dark. The fact that devils are predominantly comic figures in the modern imagination will help you. If any faint suspicion of your existence begins to arise in his mind, suggest to him a picture of something in red tights, and persuade him that since he cannot believe in that (it is an old textbook method of confusing them) he therefore cannot believe in you.

Contents

Preface

"Pastor Dean, my pastor recommended I call you. He said you deal with the demonic and may be able to help us." So, began a telephone conversation and later a series of appointments with a Christian couple whose lives were being turned upside down by the powers of darkness. *Why is their pastor sending them to me,* I mused? *Was he unable to deal with the problem, or just unwilling?* I did not address my wondering to the couple, for reasons of profession etiquette; but I have continued to wonder why many pastors are so reticent to deal with such issues? This dear couple was only one in a number of circumstances that prompted my search past the veil of darkness and into *Mission Agapé.*

Only a few months later a tragic incident hit the community in which my wife and I were ministering. The headlines of the daily newspaper were stunning and confusing. A number of community leaders had been arrested on charges of running a sexual abuse ring. Facts would come out later confirming their involvement in satanic ritual abuse (SRA). After months of investigation, the Federal Bureau of Investigation uncovered evidence of satanic rituals in and around our city of unusual proportions, including altars of blood sacrifice.

My research and study into the issues of Satan, demons,

demonic possession and spiritual warfare has not been out of morbid fascination or casual inquiry. A deep passion to see broken lives healed and areas of darkness in our community banished have been the motivation. As a father, I wanted to see my children live victoriously over things that had afflicted our families for generations. As a community leader, I longed to see areas of our city set free from the evil and wickedness that many believed to be impossible to overcome. As a counselor and pastor-teacher I longed to see lives released that seemed hopelessly gripped in addictions and phobias.

My quest has centered on a series of questions I have asked myself and others for many years. Why do some families live through the same emotional, mental and relational brokenness over generations? Could this be more than genetic predisposition, but a spiritual DNA in the family lineage? What is the root cause of people returning to addictions? Is there a deeper source of addiction than the chemicals, alcohol or pornography?

Why do some communities, regions and nations seem darker, more closed to the gospel with pastors and churches having little fruit in spite of hard work and evangelistic efforts? Why do some communities have a long history of sexual abuse, alcoholism, poverty or violence; while others have a history of peace, healthy families and prosperity? Is there a spiritual root in the history of those communities and nations that keep them bound in darkness?

Why are church leaders and the Christian community so reticent to address issues regarding Satan and his kingdom forces when it is openly addressed by Jesus Christ and the Apostles in Scripture?

These questions have been the foundation of my 30-year research into this cosmic war. Although, other questions and issues have arisen during my research, these remain the center focus and will be dealt with in the pages you are about to read.

The principles shared in these pages have not merely been born in the heart of intellectual pursuit but in the "firefight" of battle. Personal encounters with the forces of evil; hours of prayer and days of fasting for the release of precious souls from the strong grip of evil; yes, even demon possession; have been the passion and training ground of this study. As intellectual pursuit brought insight and new understanding, the question has always been: Does it work on the battlefield? Will it give more power and greater advantage when facing the malevolent forces of hell?

We are in a war of far greater proportion than most people realize. This war found its greatest expression on a rocky crag in Judea two thousand years ago. A cross with a man nailed to it was raised into the air on that small outcropping, completing the greatest mission known in the annals of history. It was a mission of love that unveiled the evil powers of darkness and set mankind free from the bondages of sin and demonic torment.

Introduction

*My dear Wormwood... It sounds as if you supposed that argument
was the way to keep him out of the Enemy's clutches. That might
have been so if he had lived a few centuries earlier. At that time the
humans still knew pretty well when a thing was proved and when it
was not; and if it was proved they really believed it. They still
connected thinking with doing and were prepared to alter their way of
life as the result of a chain of reasoning... Don't waste time trying to
make him think that materialism is true! Make him think it is
strong or stark or courageous-that is the philosophy of the future.
That's the sort of thing he cares about...*
Your affectionate uncle
Screwtape
Lewis, The Screwtape Letters

The fascination of this generation with spirits and the
occult has grown to unprecedented proportions over the
last twenty years. Simply a cursor view of the media, arts
and literature will reveal just how enamored the "Gen X,"
"Gen Y," and the "Millennial" generations have become
with the spirit world. The level of witchcraft, sorcery, and
occult portrayed in cartoons, sitcoms, movies, talk shows
and paperback books is staggering. Have you listened to
Art Bell lately, to hear the depth of interest in poltergeist,
UFO's, and other manifestations of ghouls? The search

for spiritual reality among the populace is amazing.

The media and movie industries are not the only ones who have taken the journey into this new fascination with the spirit world. Government agencies, including the military; Fortune 500 companies; and the National Education Association have been using New Age programs; like channeling, yoga, transcendental meditation, and crystals in their training sessions and classrooms. These are presented as wonderful new methods for stress relief, relaxation techniques, and conflict management.

While the media and corporate worlds have shown great interest in things of the spirit for sources of entertainment and stress management; materialism, rationalism and pragmatism are still the intellectual and philosophical base of the Western culture. The Sciences and intelligencia staunchly deny anything outside of matter. They declare that which cannot be proven or discovered by the five senses, the laws of science and through logic is not real. The spirit world is a mere fantasy and fable from their point of reference, whether it is God or devil.

Dr. Merrill F. Unger addressed this issue in his classic volume, *Biblical Demonology.*

> *Today, in an age of scientific progress and*
> *enlightenment, the most effective barrier to the*
> *adequate understanding of demonology is not*
> *a fanatical gullibility embracing mere*

superstition, but a radical skepticism rejecting
the supernatural. This obstacle of an
unbelieving rationalism is particularly
formidable, moreover, since it is widespread
among men of scholarship and learning, who
would otherwise be eminently fitted to deal
with such a field of inquiry. The seriousness
of the skeptical position is apparent when it
is considered that even a simple definition of
demonology as 'the systematic investigation of
the subject of evil spirits or demons at once
projects inquiry into the realm of the
supernatural.[i]

The denial of demonization and the existence of a real Satan is certainly not a new issue. The Apostle Paul used that very issue to disrupt a religious hearing about his rightful place to worship in the Jewish temple of Jerusalem. "And when he had so said, there are arose a dissension between the Pharisees and the Sadducees: and the multitude was divided. For the Sadducees say that there is no resurrection, neither angel, nor spirit but the Pharisees confess both." (Acts 23:7-8 KJV).

It is disturbing to see this skepticism regarding demons and evil spirits becoming firmly ensconced in evangelical and classical Pentecostal churches. The same philosophical base that prevents the secular intellegincia from accepting the spirit world has impacted many of those who claim absolute commitment to the infallibility of Scripture. They question or outright deny the working and influence of demonic and evil spirits.

Granting the fact that demon possession occurred in New Testament times, the natural question arises, 'Does it occur today?' After extensive study of demonology and years of observing patients, psychiatrist Paul Meier gives his professional opinion:

> *I can honestly say that I have never yet seen a single case of demon possession. The main thing I have learned about demon possession is how little we really know about it and how little the Bible says about it.*
>
> *… Don't get me wrong. I am a strict Biblicist who believes in the inerrancy of Scripture. I believe demons really do exist because the Bible says they do. I believe that there probably are some demon possessed persons in various parts of the world.[ii]*

With this kind of reasoning, one must ask whether Jesus' command to go and cast out demons in His name is no longer part of the Great Commission given to the church. Is it no longer relevant? Indeed, has the Western culture become so educated and advanced that Satan and his demons can no longer do their work? Have they ceased to exist or must they concentrate their efforts in other countries that are not so advanced?

The late Malcolm Muggeridge put it this way in his classic writing, *Jesus, the Man Who Lives.*

> *Even those who are prepared in a vague way*
> *to acknowledge the existence of a deity draw*
> *the line at the devil. A Creator of the*
> *universe and planner of its and our destinies*
> *who wound up the evolutionary process in the*
> *first place and then left it to unwind itself -*
> *yes, just conceivable; but a devil representing*
> *the contrary principle, destructive rather than*
> *creative, malevolent rather than beneficent, is*
> *another matter, and quite out of the question.*
> *Personally, I have found the devil easier to*
> *believe in than God; for one thing, alas, I*
> *have had more to do with him. It seems to me*
> *quite extraordinary that anyone should have*
> *failed to notice, especially during the last half-*
> *century, a diabolic presence in the world,*
> *pulling downwards as gravity does instead of*
> *pressing upwards as trees and plants do when*
> *they grow and reach so resolutely and*
> *beautifully after the light. A counter-force to*
> *creativity; destructive in its nature and*
> *purpose, raging far and wide like a forest fire,*
> *and burning in the heart's core - pinpointed*
> *there, a fiery tongue of fierce desire. Have we*
> *not seen this devil's destructiveness making a*

bonfire of past, present and future in one
mighty conflagration? Smelt him, rancid-
sweet? Touched him, slippery-soft? Measured
with the eye of his fearful shape. Heard his
fearful rhetoric? Glimpsed him, sometimes in
a mirror, with drooling, greedy mouth, misty
ravening eyes and flushed flesh? Who can
miss him in those blackest of all moments,
when God seems to have disappeared, leaving
the devil to occupy an empty universe?[iii]

In a culture with a growing preoccupation for the occult
and the "nether world," these issues are becoming more
relevant. It is incumbent upon the church to have a ready
answer that makes sense and brings truth to the issues.

There is no more salient point than the recent *Harry Potter*
craze. This series of books created by the English
authoress, J. K. Rowling, has sold more than one hundred
million copies in two hundred nations around the world.
The first book in this series that charts the adventures of a
young orphan with magical powers has been translated
into forty-two languages. Young readers and even the
authoress, herself, have clearly stated it is an open war
between the kingdom of Satan and the kingdom of God.

"Jesus died because He was weak and stupid." This is a quote
from 6-year-old Jessica Lehman of Easley, SC, after
reading the *Harry Potter* books!

A quote from Hartland, WI, 10-year-old Craig Nowell, a recent convert to the New Satanic Order of the Black Circle: *"The Harry Potter books are cool, 'cause they teach you all about magic and how you can use it to control people and get revenge on your enemies. I want to learn the Cruciatus Curse, to make my muggle science teacher suffer for giving me a D."* (A muggle is an unbeliever in magic.

Here is Ashley, a 9-year-old, the typical average age reader of *Harry Potter*. *"I used to believe in what they taught us at Sunday School,"* said Ashley, conjuring up an ancient spell to summon Cerebus, the three headed hound of hell. *"But the Harry Potter books showed me that magic is real, something I can learn and use right now, and that the Bible is nothing but boring lies."*

... And finally, a quote from the author, herself ... describing the objections of Christian reviewers to her writings: *"I think it's absolute rubbish to protest children's books on the grounds that they are luring children to Satan. People should be praising them for that! These books guide children to an understanding that the weak, idiotic Son of God is a living hoax who will be humiliated when the rain of fire comes ...while we, his faithful servants, laugh and cavort in victory."*[iv]

The line has been drawn in the sand. We are at war! This is not a time for appeasement or negotiation. We find ourselves, spiritually, in the same place Great Britain was in May 13, 1940. Lord Neville Chamberlain had been in negotiations with Adolph Hitler for months. Following each meeting the Nazi regime held more of mainland Europe; first, the east banks of the Rhine River. Next, Austria was annexed under German control. Sudetenland was invaded after the Munich Accord in 1938. September 1, 1939, Poland came under the heel of the Jackboot and the stunning power of the blitzkrieg. In response to the invasion of Poland, England and France declared war on Germany.

The whole of Europe was living under the fear of the "broken cross." Lord Chamberlain was replaced, as Prime Minister, of Britain by the "Bull Dog," after the months of inept leadership. May 13th, Sir Winston Churchill gave his first address to the Parliament of Britain. In part, the halls of that great chamber resounded with these stunning words.

> ... I would say to the house, as I have said
> to those who have joined this government: 'I
> have nothing to offer but blood, toil, tears and
> sweat.' We have before us an ordeal of the
> most grievous kind. We have before us many,
> many long months of struggle and of suffering.
> You ask, what is our policy? I will say: it is
> to wage war, by sea, land and air, with all
> our might and with all the strength that God
> can give us: to wage war against a monstrous
> tyranny never surpassed in the dark
> lamentable catalogue of human crime. That is

our policy. You ask what is our aim? I can
answer in one word: Victory. Victory, at all
cost. Victory, in spite of all terror. Victory,
however long and hard the road may be; for
without victory, there is no survival. Let that
be realized; no survival for the British
Empire; no survival for all that the British
Empire has stood for, no survival for the urge
and impulses of the ages, that mankind will
move forward towards its goal. But I take up
my task with buoyancy and hope. I feel sure
that our cause will not be suffered to fail
among men. At this time, I feel entitled to
claim the aid of all, and I say, 'Come, then,
let us go forward together with our united
strength.[v]

Six days after Sir Winston Churchill had given that moving speech to the Parliament he spoke to his nation on public radio, "Our task is not only to win the battle- but to win the war."[vi]

That is the task before the church. We must take up arms - spiritual arms that are "mighty through God to the pulling down of strongholds" (2 Cor.10:3-4). We must go forward doing great exploits for the kingdom of God, extending the mission Jesus Christ accomplished on the cross to the ends of the earth.

We must see victory!

Victory through the cross of Christ!

Victory by the blood of the Lamb and the word of our testimony!

Victory by our faith!

Without victory there will be no survival for mankind!

We must unveil the mask of darkness and set the captives free!

We must complete *Mission Agape*!

A Declaration of War

My dear Wormwood,

… All sorts of virtues painted in the fantasy or approved by the intellect or even, in some measure, loved and admired, will not keep a man from Our Father's House: indeed, they may make him more amusing when he gets there.

Your affectionate Uncle

Screwtape

Lewis The Screwtape Letters

It must have appeared like a scene right out of a horror movie, to those who were watching a three-hundred-pound man, slithering across a living room floor on his back, like a snake. His tongue was darting in and out of his mouth like a serpent. Kneeling over the man, I began doing the only thing I could imagine in that situation. I commanded demons to leave him in the name of Jesus Christ. Unexpectedly, the man began to yell loudly, "Abaddon! Abaddon! Help me, Abaddon! Abaddon!"

Two hours passed, seeming like mere moments, as I wrestled with the demonic forces driving that giant of a man. He returned to his right mind; asked God to forgive him for the evil things he had done and for the specific sin that had brought him to that encounter.

Questions were flooding my mind during the ride back north on I-5, that summer morning of 1980. The friends with me on that trip were very animated as they peppered me with questions about the all the things they had just witnessed.

How does that happen, Pastor? How was he able to act like a snake? Were you afraid when all of that was happening? Did you feel some kind of supernatural power as you held that giant of man down with one hand, while you were driving out the demons? Who was Abaddon?

"Indeed, I thought, "how does that kind of thing happen and who was Abaddon?" I was asking myself some of those same questions and knew I would be spending a lot of time over the next weeks and months searching for the answers.

Authority as Stewards

God made a covenant of great blessing when He created the first human beings.

> *And God blessed them, and God said unto them, "Be*
> *fruitful, multiply, replenish the earth, subdue it and have*
> *dominion over the fish of the sea, and over the fowl of the*
> *air, and over every living thing that moveth upon the earth."*
> *(Genesis 1:28 KJV).*

Clearly, it was God's intent for mankind to be the steward of his new creation. The covenant promise gave mankind authority to do four things.

Mankind was to be fruitful and prosperous in all that he put his hand to do. God meant for him to multiply; that is to procreate and fill the earth with humankind. He was to replenish the earth. Mankind is to serve as steward of the natural resources of the earth; including mineral, plant, fowl, fish, and animal life. He was to subdue it and have dominion. Mankind was given authority and power to be the ruler of earth.

The magnitude of authority God gave mankind to rule planet earth is revealed in Psalm 8:4-8 and in Hebrews 2:6-8. God left nothing on planet earth that was not put under the authority and rule of man. The Psalmist said, "Thou madest him to have dominion over the works of Thy hands; Thou hast put all things under his feet" (Ps. 8:6). Adam and his lineage were to be the ambassadors of God's kingdom on the earth. In the authority of God's Name, mankind would extend the rule of His law and the power of His Kingdom throughout all the earth.

God chose His words carefully when He wrote the covenant with Adam and Eve; telling them to *subdue it* and *have dominion*. Those are strong terms, expressing power to crush an enemy. Why would God use such terms in His covenant with the original couple? Because there was an enemy to be conquered and mankind would have the responsibility of displacing the enemy from the regions and atmosphere of planet earth.

The War of Heaven

War had been declared against the throne and the kingdom of God, by one of the angels. At some point in time, previous to the creation events recorded in Genesis chapters one and two, Lucifer, the covering Cherub rebelled against the authority and rule of the Almighty. He decided to establish himself as god. "How art thou fallen from heaven, O Lucifer, son of the morning! How art thou cut down to the ground, which didst weaken the nations! For thou hast said in thine heart, I will ascend into heaven, I will exalt my throne above the stars of God: I will sit also upon the mount of the congregation, in the sides of the north: I will ascend above the heights of the clouds; I will be like the Most High." (Isaiah 14:12-17)

Ezekiel 28:11-19 record the words and the actions of Lucifer's rebellion.

> *Thou art the anointed cherub that covereth; and I have set thee so: thou wast upon the holy mountain of God; thou hast walked up and down in the midst of the stones of fire. Thou wast perfect in thy ways from the day that thou wast created, till iniquity was found in thee. Thine heart was lifted up because of thy beauty, thou hast corrupted thy wisdom by reason of thy brightness: I will cast thee to the ground, I will lay thee before kings, that they may behold thee.*

There are those who question the validity of applying these passages of Scripture to the Luciferic rebellion. They would attribute them only as a historical record of Babylon and Tyre. Other passages of the Holy Writings, however, reveal there are "shadow powers" behind the historical working of governments and nations (Daniel 10:2-21). Dr. Ed Murphy agrees, saying these chapters are "consistent with the biblical picture of Satan and his fallen angels." He goes on to say in his definitive volume, *The Handbook for Spiritual Warfare* (Nashville. Thomas Nelson, 1992):

> *When we come to the New Testament, however, the picture is much clearer. We are not left with mere hints of cosmic rebellion. Instead the New Testament declares that such rebellion did occur. From the*

Revelation 12:4 reveals a third of the angels followed Lucifer in his rebellion against the living God. Jude described this rebellion as angels "who kept not their first estate but left their own habitation" (Jude 6). These angelic beings were not content with the position and assignments given to them from the gracious and just Creator of all things. They desired more. They were greedy for more power, greater position and more authority. In their pride and ambition, they chose to follow Lucifer in his rebellion against the Almighty. God would have none of it. As any wise and just magistrate, Lord of Hosts not only removed them from position and power, He cast them out of Heaven to the atmosphere of planet earth.

After the rebellion these fallen angels established their own kingdom, with Lucifer as their commander. They set themselves to fight against God and His Kingdom, in every place, in every way and by every means possible.

There was no question in the mind of Jesus Christ about this "shadow power" existing and working on planet earth. He and His cousin, John the Baptist believed these forces must be confronted and displaced. Their sermons consisted of "Repent, for the kingdom of heaven is at hand" (Matthew 3:2; 4:17). The whole purpose of their ministry was to bring the power and authority of the kingdom of heaven against the kingdom of darkness.

Jesus Christ encountered the Prince of Darkness face to face following His baptism by John the Baptist in the Jordan River (Matthew 4:1-11). When

Jesus sent the twelve disciples out to minister to the lost sheep of Israel, He commanded them to preach "the kingdom of heaven is at hand" (Matthew 10:7). The same command was given to the seventy other disciples Jesus sent to the communities He was going to visit (Luke 10:9).

Jesus gave a very similar command to the church in Mark 16:15-18. The Apostolic church carried out the orders of their Commander in Chief. Wherever they found the "shadowy powers" of darkness they confronted them and displaced them. Acts 5:16 documents the Apostles healed many who had unclean spirits. Philip, the deacon turned evangelist went to Samaria and preached the Gospel. He delivered many who were possessed with unclean spirits (Acts 8:7). The Apostle Paul and his evangelistic team went to the city of Philippi. A demon possessed girl continually interrupted the meetings. The Apostle Paul cast a demon out of the girl (Acts 16:16-20). The church at Ephesus had a powerful ministry against evil spirits (Acts 19:12).

A Very Real Devil Exists

Lucifer has become known by many names in this war. These names are often mocked. But be assured, Lucifer is not a joke. He is not a comic book character. He is very real, very powerful and very evil. His names describe his role and work.

Lucifer was his angelic name meaning "the bearer of light." He was the covering Cherub around the throne of God (Isaiah 14:12, Ezekiel 28:14). The Apostle Paul referred to the deceiving power of Lucifer's image in 2 Corinthians 11:14-15, "And no marvel; for Satan himself is transformed into an angel of light. Therefore, it is no great thing if his ministers also be transformed as the ministers of righteousness; whose end shall be according to their works" (KJV)

The Scripture refers to him as the devil (Matthew 4:5). The Greek word is *diabolos*, a false accuser. The Book of Revelation describes his work as follows:

> *Now have come the salvation and the power and the kingdom of our*
> *God, and the authority of his Christ. For the accuser of our*
> *brothers, who accuses them before our God day and night, has been*
> *hurled down (Revelation 12:10 KJV).*

He is also referred to as Satan; meaning the adversary in Hebrew (Job 1:6) and in Greek (Matthew 4:10). The Apostle Peter said, "Be sober, be vigilant; because your adversary the devil, as a roaring lion, walketh about, seeking whom he may devour" (1 Peter 5:8).

The Dragon is another name for our adversary. The Apostle John described the scene. "And war broke out in heaven: Michael and his angels fought with the dragon; and the dragon and his angels fought" (Revelation 12:7).

He is also the Serpent - *nachash* in Hebrew and *ophis* in Greek both words mean a snake.

> *Now the serpent was more subtle than any beast of the field which*
> *the LORD God had made. And he said unto the woman, Yea,*
> *hath God said, Ye shall not eat of every tree of the garden (Genesis*
> *3:1).*

The Scribes and the Pharisees called him Beelzebub which means the Lord of the house or the prince.

> *But some of them said, "He casts out demons by Beelzebub, the ruler of the demons." (Matthew 12:24).*

He is also called Abaddon and Apollyon, the destroyer or one of destruction. They had as king over them the angel of the Abyss, whose name in Hebrew is Abaddon, and in Greek, Apollyon (Revelation 9:11 NIV).

The Call to Arms

As a result of this coupe, God delegated Adam and Eve with the authority to wage war, as stewards of His new creation. There was no question whether there would be an attack by the forces of darkness against the new ambassadors of the kingdom of light. Pride and ambition, resident in the heart of the evil one, would not allow those created in the very image of God to abide unchallenged in the Garden of Eden, for very long. It was only a matter of time and by what means the attack would come. He must take the conflict to them. The war with God must rise to a new level, taking on whole new proportions. The war would now enter into the hearts of men.

A Matter of Treason

My dear Wormwood,

The most alarming thing in your last account of the patient is that he is making none of those confident resolutions which marked his original conversion...I see only one thing to do at the moment. Your patient has become humble; have you drawn his attention to the fact? All virtues are less formidable to us once the man is aware that he has them, but this is specially true of humility. Catch him at the moment when he is really poor in spirit and smuggle into his mind the gratifying reflection, "By jove! I'm being humble," and almost immediately pride - pride at his own humility - will appear. If he awakes to the danger and tries to smother this new form of pride, make him proud of his attempt-and so on, through as many stages as you please. . . .

Your Affectionate Uncle,

Screwtape

Lewis, The Screwtape Letters

I wondered in amazement as a precious United Church of Canada pastor told me his story. He was a graduate of an Ivy League school of theology. He led services in the traditional liturgy of the high church. He also held informal Bible studies through the week, giving people opportunity to experience genuine salvation and other works of grace.

"I have a psychologist in town that sends people to me for deliverance," he said casually. "He realizes there are cases that cannot be explained or helped by psychology," He intoned, "So, he writes out a prescription for the people to come see me. When they arrive with a prescription from his office, I know what he is suspecting. They probably have a demon and need some level of deliverance."

I did not know what to say. I believed demons were real. I had even encountered them during a bone chilling experience while conducting meetings in a small Pentecostal church in the Pacific Northwest of the United States. The memories of that encounter were too vivid, even as I sat listening to this pastor's story, more than three years later.

The service was over. Everyone had left the building but me. Suddenly, a presence filled the room. "We will kill you," declared the sonorous voice. Chills went over my whole body, as I looked in the direction from which the voice had come. No one was there. But, the voice was audible. "We will destroy you," He cried again. It was then I realized the room was filled with evil spirits. They surrounded me with an evil intent. "Lord Jesus what shall I do?" I could not speak. I could hardly think. The words, "Command them to leave" flooded my mind. "Be bold! Take authority in My name and by My blood!" Out of my mouth came a bold and authoritative voice commanding the demonic forces to leave the building. Suddenly, the outside doors opened and closed, without human agent. The dark presence was gone.

"You do believe in demon possession and deliverance, don't you? That is part of your denominations beliefs, isn't it," the Pastor inquired; bringing me back to the conversation we were having. "Yes," I answered, wondering when the last time was that I had heard of anyone who took deliverance from demonic possession seriously; let alone practiced it as a regular part of their ministry. The impact this precious man of God had on the community was undeniable. He was not only well known but dearly loved and respected by community leaders and residents, alike. I left our lunch meeting questioning, "How will I deal with these important spiritual issues?"

The Tragedy of Defeat

We are not told in Holy Writ how long the couple abode in their paradise before the malevolent evil came slithering into the pristine setting. No documentation is given to the number of satanic encounters, if indeed there were others, previous to the devious meeting between the bride of Adam and the satanic serpent, recorded in the third chapter of Genesis.

The subtlety and stealth with which the serpent approached the woman is only matched by the tragedy of her yielding to the lure of pride and the enticement her husband into the same rebellious act. Dr. Murphy says,

> *There seem to be only three major ways of viewing the serpent's role*
> *in the temptation story. First is to see it literally… Second is to*
> *view it allegorically… The third manner of viewing the story is both*
> *literal and symbolic… The events involving Adam and Eve*
> *actually happened the way Moses records them. He does, however,*
> *use symbolism to tell his story (The Handbook for Spiritual*
> *Warfare)*

This devilish encounter was repeated four thousand years later on a Judean mountain, with dramatically different results. The battlefield and the pugilists were different, but the objective was the same. The serpent, the devil, came tempting the Last Adam, Jesus Christ; to use His powers to turn a rock into bread; tempt God by telling Him to throw Himself off the temple; worship him and he would give Him the kingdoms of the world. The Son of Man humbled Himself to God and resisted the devil, instead of being lifted up in pride. He sent the Prince of Darkness away, rather than yielding to his enticement. Angels then came and ministered to the Son of God who had just defeated the enemy (Matthew 4:1-11).

The account in Genesis three has a very different outcome. The Satan-filled serpent found fertile soil to win a great battle, *but not the war.* The tragic outcome of Adam's defeat was soon revealed.

"Treason, Treason, Treason," must have resounded through the heavens, as all of creation began experiencing the impact of mankind's betrayal. God's stewards had yielded to the bribery of hell's secret agent.

Creator God knew immediately of the traitorous act and "came walking in the garden in the cool of the day," to meet them and give His stewards grace and the opportunity to confess and repent of their actions (Genesis 3:8). "Adam, where are you," called the Sovereign of all creation. Adam answered, "I heard Your voice in the garden, and I was afraid because I was naked; and I hid myself." And He said, "Who told you that you were naked? Have you eaten from the tree of which I commanded you that you should not eat?" (Genesis 3:10-11 NKJV).

Adam's response is very revealing, "The woman, whom you gave to be with me, she…" There was no repentance in his heart. Blame shifting and pride were expressed, as Adam refused to take personal responsibility (Genesis 3:8-12). The immediate effects of the sin are at least sevenfold.

The first is shame. Adam and Eve are embarrassed and ashamed of their nakedness. They make a hasty effort to cover themselves using fig leaves.

The second is separation from God. Adam and Eve loved spending time with Heavenly Father previous to this horrible event. The guilt in their heart caused them to hide from His presence. The lack of honesty before God was the third. Blame shifting was the fourth effect. The fifth was immediate judgment upon the man and his wife. Forced separation from the Paradise of God came next. The existence of ongoing spiritual warfare was the seventh effect.

A Power Shift

Genesis 3:15 is one of the most critical and controversial passages in all of Scripture. It reveals three principles which will dominate planet earth for all of human history. God said, "And I will put enmity between you and the woman, and between your seed and her seed; He shall bruise you on the head, And you shall bruise him on the heel" (NAS).

The basic nature of mankind changed from righteousness to sinfulness bringing with it death and separation from God. A major power shift took place when Adam and Eve sinned and spiritual warfare filled man's existence all of his days on earth. The time would come when the "Seed of Woman" would enter the human race and win the spiritual war.

"You shall bruise him on the heel" is reference to the authority shift that took place through Adam's treason. Lucifer became the "prince of the power of the air" (Eph. 2:2) and "the god of this world" (2 Cor. 4:4). He and his fallen angels established themselves as "the rulers of the darkness of this world, the spiritual wickedness in high places" (Eph. 6:12). As a result, the "Cosmic War" would be fought on three fronts.

13

The Battlefield of the Human Mind and Flesh

The hearts and the flesh of mankind would be used by Satan and his demons to control and to destroy individuals. The Apostle Paul described it well in Ephesians 2:1-3.

> *And you were dead in your trespasses and sins, in which you formerly walked according to the course of this world, according to the prince of the power of the air, of the spirit that is now working in the sons of disobedience. Among them we too all formerly lived in the lusts of our flesh, indulging the desires of the flesh and of the mind, and were by nature children of wrath, even as the rest (NAS).*

God had warned Adam and Eve if they partook of the tree of the knowledge of good and evil they would die (Genesis 2:17). The reality of that truth became all too clear. The Apostle Paul wrote to the church in Rome, "Therefore, just as through one man sin entered into the world, and death through sin, and thus death spread to all men. (Romans 5:12 KJV)

Why would death spread to all men? The sin nature of Adam passed to his sons and then to all mankind. "There is none righteous, no not one. For all have sinned and come short of the glory of God." (Romans 3:10, 23 KJV).

The impact of this truth was realized all too quickly in the first family. Cain, filled with self-will and jealousy, murdered his brother, Able (Genesis 4:1-8). The sin of Cain was then passed to his generations (Genesis 4:12). God said,

14

"When you till the ground it shall no longer yield its strength to you. A fugitive and a vagabond you shall be in the earth."

The effect of sin is visible in every generation of the human race. History records one long story of selfishness, greed, jealousy, murder, and wars. All are manifestations of the sinful nature of man, dogging him from birth through his death.

The Battlefield of Cultures and Social Orders

Cultures and social orders have become major areas of strongholds as Satan seeks to control regions and nations with his demonic powers.

Man's sinful heart had an immediate impact upon the social order and the culture of the early human race. Demonic forces sought to capitalize upon the fallen nature, by cohabiting with women to corrupt the culture and the social order even further, as recorded in Genesis 6:1-4.

> *Now it came to pass, when men began to multiply upon the face of the earth, and daughters were born to them, that the sons of God saw the daughters of men, that they were beautiful; and took wives for themselves of all whom they chose. And there were giants on the earth in those days and also afterward, when the sons of God came into the daughters of men and they bore children to them. Those were the mighty men who were of old, men of renown.*

The results were devastating to mankind and society, "When every imagination of the heart was only evil continually" (Genesis 6:5), resulting in the flood of the earth and the destruction of mankind and his depraved culture.

The godly family of Noah was spared, through whom the "Seed of Woman" would come. Again, Satan attacked the society and culture of the human race. This time he filled the hearts of man with pride to exalt themselves and reach to heaven with the Tower of Babel. God judged mankind by confusing their language and spreading them throughout the earth.

George Otis, Jr. spent seven years, traveling in almost fifty countries, tracing the Babel Pump and researching the spiritual effects upon the cultures and social orders of the world. Rev. Otis' research centered on the question, "Why does spiritual darkness linger where it does?"[7] Tracing the Semites, Hamites, and Japhethites, Otis followed them through their journeys to the four corners of the compass and into every continent. Record was found of the routes and patterns used by the people groups, as they crossed the ranges and settled new lands.

> *In the centuries that followed, the descendants of these early emigrants spread and even Eden traveled with them, these tended to fade the farther they traveled from the land of their origin. To preserve their connection to the past, many aboriginal peoples developed a collection of core myths that could be passed conveniently to succeeding generations. A mixture of factual history and human imagination, these myths were bound by two closely related themes: the golden age and Ancient Wisdom.[8]*

George discovered a common theme in the journey of every people group is

"each of these ancient peoples encountered some form of *collective trauma.* . ..
Regardless of whether Satan caused these circumstances or simply took
advantage of them, their effect was to provide him a direct entrance into the
psyches of otherwise distracted people. It was a perfect setup."

Satan would seize the opportunities to establish strongholds in the hearts and
the culture of people. From these strongholds he would bind them to
behavior patterns and cravings contrary to God. History records there are
occasions when the Word of God would come to cities and nations leading
them to repentance and deliverance, like Jonah and Nineveh.

> *Unfortunately, the sackcloth prostrations of Nineveh have proven a
> rare exception to historical rule. The overwhelming majority of
> people down through the centuries have elected to exchange the
> relations of God for a lie. Heeding the entreaties of demons, they
> have chosen in their desperation to enter into intimate compacts with
> the spirit world. In return for the consent of a particular deity to
> resolve their immediate traumas, they have collectively sold their
> proverbial souls.*
>
> *Through just such agreements, demonic forces were authorized to
> establish territorial strongholds during the long sojourn out from
> Babel. The basis of these transactions was (and is) entirely moral.
> People made conscious choices to suppress the truth and believe a
> falsehood. In the end, as Romans 1:18-25 reminds us, the people
> were deceived because they chose to be.*[9]

Satan has continually sought to destroy God, His kingdom, and mankind by
corrupting nations, cultures and society. It can be seen in the history of the

Egyptian, Assyrian, Babylonian, Mede and Persian, Grecian, and Roman empires. Each one reached an amazing zenith of power, architecture, literature and art. What remains today are only hollow shells of their great halls, filled with weeds and trees, in which the wind howls. They are stark testimonies of self-destruction, over indulgence and the sensuality of man's sinful nature.

The question begs to be asked, "Is there any hope for mankind?" The answer resounds from the Garden of Eden, "I will put enmity between you and the woman, and between your seed and her seed. He shall bruise your head and you shall bruise His heel."

From the very beginning, when the original stewards fell into sin, God promised there would be hope through the "Seed of Woman" who would crush Satan and his demonic kingdom. That is the third arena of Genesis 3:15.

The War of Two Kingdoms and the Church

Almighty God declared war in Genesis 3:15; setting up the conflict between the kingdom of God and the kingdom of Satan. This conflagration would dominate the history of mankind. This spiritual warfare will continue until death has finally been put under the feet of Jesus Christ, forever. Then Satan and his demonic hosts will be cast into the Lake of Fire and the kingdom of God will be established under the authority of Heavenly Father. 1 Corinthians 15:24-28 and Revelation 20:10-14 declare these events. The Apostle Paul urged the church at Ephesus, "For our struggle is not against flesh and blood, but against the rulers, against the powers, against the world forces of this darkness, against the spiritual {forces} of wickedness in the heavenly {places}. Therefore, take up the full armor of God that you may be able to resist in the evil day, and having done everything, to stand firm" (Ephesians 6:12-13 NAS).

Satan, death and hell will rule over mankind and planet earth until the "Seed of Woman" crushes his head and destroys his power. The whole history of the human race centers upon the coming "Seed of Woman" and Satan's war the kingdom of God through mankind. Jesus Christ who is the "Seed of Woman" and the source of our victory said, "The thief comes only to steal, and kill, and destroy; I came that they might have life, and might have {it} abundantly" (John 10:10 NAS).

A Conflict of Worldviews

My dear Wormwood,

. . . The two churches nearest to him, I have looked up in the office. Both have certain claims. At the first of these the vicar is a man who has been so long engaged in watering down the faith to make it easier for a supposedly incredulous and hardheaded congregation that it is now he who shocks his parishioners with his unbelief, not vice versa. He has undermined many a soul's Christianity. . . ..

Your affectionate Uncle

Screwtape

Lewis, The Screwtape Letters

I was in the early years of completing my undergraduate work, taking my third course in psychology. It was a lab. My responsibility was to conduct a counseling session then have the professor critique my work following each of the sessions. It was during this time an important question began troubling my mind.

"How do you counsel a demon?", the question came. "What?", I thought to myself. "Exactly how do you go about counseling a demon?", the thought came again. My mind went back to the conversation with the Canadian pastor and the encounter with the demonized giant of a man. I reviewed the theories and presuppositions of psychology. "How would you go about counseling a demon?", came the persistent thought. The realization of God's challenge slowly dawned in my heart. I was in a conflict of two world views. Would I believe God's Word or place my confidence in the ideology and the philosophy of men? It is a conflict that has faced the people of God for centuries. Paul faced it when he addressed the "men of Athens" in the Areopagus about man's sinfulness and need for a Savior.

> *Therefore, since we are God's offspring, we should not think that*
> *the divine being is like gold or silver or stone-an image made by*
> *man's design and skill. In the past God overlooked such ignorance,*
> *but now he commands all people everywhere to repent. For he has*
> *set a day when he will judge the world with justice by the man he*
> *has appointed. He has given proof of this to all men by raising him*
> *from the dead. (Acts 17:16-31).*

The Apostle faced it again when he was called before the Sanhedrin. The Sadducees did not believe in angels and demons but the Pharisees did (Acts 23:6-10). These same issues are being wrestled by this generation of the church.

A Matter of Truth

It is a fundamental matter of whose truth the church will believe. Will the church accept the principles of God's Word regarding mankind and the spirit world or will the church accept the materialistic, rationalistic and humanistic view commonly held today? These models of man and the world are not compatible but opposing views of the origin, basic nature, and need of the human race.

Their basic presuppositions of the human race greatly differ. Rogers, Skinner and Freud developed psychological models and presuppositions of mankind, believing him to be basically good.[10]

The Biblical principles teach otherwise. According to God's Word, man is not basically good but sinners by nature. This was the lament of King David, "Behold, I was brought forth in iniquity, and in sin my mother conceived me."[11] Left to himself, without divine intervention, the human race will self-destruct through moral corruption. The Apostle Paul declared in Romans 7:18-19 "For I know that in me (that is, in my flesh) nothing good dwells; for to will is present with me, but how to perform what is good I do not find. For the good that I will to do, I do not do; but the evil I will not to do, that I practice" (NKJV)

Gary Collins, in his book *Search for Reality*, lists those models of mankind that oppose the Biblical model.

> *While there are many existing opinions about man's nature, both within the field of psychology and without, we will limit our consideration to five of the most commonly held viewpoints.*
>
> *1. The mechanical view of man. Sometimes called the "naturalistic view…"*
>
> *2. The biological view of man. Closely related to the mechanical view is the position that man is primarily a complex… animal…*
>
> *3. The culturalistic view of man. This view states that a man's nature is largely molded by society…*

4. The humanistic view. Regards man as basically good,
rational, self-sufficient, able to control his own future…

5. The existential view of man. Man is basically restless,
anxious, insecure and struggling to find meaning in life…
Hopeless…[12]

The acceptance of a spiritual basis to life and culture is adamantly challenged by those with a materialistic and rationalistic world view. The Scriptures accept such a view without question. "While we do not look at the things which are seen, but at the things which are not seen. For the things which are seen are temporary, but the things which are not seen are eternal."[13] The writer of Hebrews declared, "By faith we understand that the worlds were framed by the word of God, so that the things which are seen were not made of things which are visible."[14] The reality of angels and demons and the involvement of the Father, Son and Holy Spirit in the lives of human beings is a basic presupposition of Scripture (Luke 1:26-37; Matthew 12:22-32; John 14:1-31).

These opposing ideologies make it difficult, almost impossible, for the church in the Western world to establish a ministry paradigm that deals with the kingdom of darkness. There is constant pressure to take a middle ground that compromises the basic biblical view of life.

The Twilight Labyrinth deals with things that are real, but not
seen; with things that are hinted at, but not broadcast. While
nonwestern readers will nod knowingly at the following stories and
concepts, those from rationalist-oriented cultures will occasionally

stumble. Taught to avow a clear split between the spiritual and the material, most Westerners are uncomfortable with the supernatural as an everyday companion. As the late writer Anais Nin once said, "We don't see things as they are; we see them as we are." Our own experiences (or lack of them) have a profound effect on the way we view the external world.

As the torrent of daily life rushes past us we use these experiences to filter out an astonishing volume of ideological flotsam and jetsam. Reality is whatever gets through.[15]

Everyone holds a world view based upon life experience, family training, community, culture and education. The challenge facing the Christian believer is to match their worldview to the principles and precepts of God's Word, not the other way around.

Aside from the agnostic position, only two conceivable world views exist. The spiritualistic world view affirms that ultimate reality is spiritual; immaterial, not physical or material. According to this view, whether ultimate reality is looked upon as personal or impersonal it is spiritual. . ..

Second the materialistic or naturalistic world view affirms that ultimate reality is material or physical not spiritual. This view assumes all life began spontaneously from nonlife and that by this process primitive single-celled life forms evolved over vast periods of time into the vast range of life as know it today.

Five important conclusions result from this view of reality.

1. The universe is a cosmic accident that has no ultimate purpose.

2. Human life is a biological accident that has no ultimate significance.

3. Life ends forever at death for each individual life form.

4. Mind has no separate existence or survival apart from brain.

5. Humanity's intuitive, historic belief in an ultimate mind, spirit, or God behind, within and outside of the physical universe is a form of self-deception. Thus, humanity's corresponding belief in human uniqueness, dignity, purpose, and survival beyond death is a non-real view of reality. . ..

Western theology has been influenced by the Western world view more than most of us are aware. By Western theology I mean the broad, generally accepted interpretations of Scripture embodied in mainstream works of systematic theology, covering the broad range of theological viewpoints and ecclesiastical groupings one finds among all believers who hold to a high view of Scripture and propagate a common historic Christian faith.

By Western world view I mean the view of reality that arose out of the historical movement of the eighteenth century called the enlightenment. . . .

How does all of this affect our study of spiritual war? Although we Christians have rightly rejected naturalism as an acceptable view of ultimate reality and hold faithfully to historic theism, naturalism nonetheless deeply influences our view of the daily events of our lives. This influence helps shape our view of the world of spirit beings, both benevolent and evil.[16]

Anthropologist, Paul G. Hiebert, of Trinity Evangelical Divinity School and former missionary to India, wrote of his struggles with this world view conflict in an article entitled *"The Flaw of the Excluded Middle."* In the article he described *"A Western Two-tiered View of Reality"*[17] in which faith and science are viewed as two different realities and do not mix. It is a Western type of dualism.

What has been excluded in this Christian Western view of reality is the practice of witchcraft, shamans, idols, household gods, and other spirit powers. These have been relegated to folk lore and fables. Western culture enjoys them as entertainment in movies, television and stage. They are not accepted as a part of reality. Western theology, with its roots in the logic and rationalism of the Enlightenment, allows no room for the supernatural work of the demonic. Otis says, *"The Acts of the Apostles has given way to the Enlightenment."*[18]

Sickness and disease are explained through the science of medicine. Emotional and mental disorders are analyzed through the science of psychology and psychiatry. Addictions and behavioral dysfunction are perceived and aided through the medical model of social sciences. No room is made for the spirit realm.

> *Dr. Francis Schaffer presented a pleasant exception to the trend in his 1972 book, Genesis in Space and Time. As he saw it, the supernatural world is the intriguing half of the universe, one that stands 'not somewhere afar off, but immediately before us almost as a fourth dimension.' To Schaeffer, this fact carries significant implications. Not only does humanity live in the fold of the supernatural realm, he believed, but there is cause and effect relationship between it and our own visible world at every existential moment.[19]*

A major shift is taking place in the Western culture; a virtual explosion of the occult and Spiritism. Globalization has brought the Eastern culture and its world view into the Western universities and media. Their influence has been felt at every level of Western civilization and brought wide acceptance of the "excluded middle." This will continue to bring greater and greater pressure upon the Christian church to reexamine its worldview and the reality of evil spirits and their influence upon everyday living.

These issues are taken for granted in both the Old and New Testaments, especially so in the New Testament. Jesus addressed demonic influence in every aspect of daily life; sickness, disease, mental and behavioral disorders, and relational dysfunction were all addressed from the view of demonic influence.

Apostolic ministry addressed life from the same perspective. The Apostle Paul urged the believers in Ephesus to live in the power of resurrection life and not practice their old lifestyles of lying, stealing, cursing, bitterness and hate. He included in the list, "neither give place to the devil" (Ephesians. 4:27).

The Western Church must reexamine the reality of the "excluded middle" and the kingdom of darkness. She must accept the responsibility for addressing these issues biblically and accurately if she is to assist the Western culture, indeed, the whole of mankind to win the war.

The occult practices and evil powers of darkness, once believed only to exist in the jungles of the far off mission fields, have entered the homes and living rooms of America and Western Europe. They have come by way of television, videos and computer games. They have become play things in the children's toy boxes. They fill the books our children read and they are the super heroes of the cartoons our children watch. Deformed physical appearances (i.e. tattoos, facial and body piercing, nose bones, enlarged ear lobes and pierced tongues) once confined to the tribal customs of demonized jungles, have become the rage of fashion for Western youth and young adults.

Questions, once thought to be extreme or begging the question, must be addressed. What is the role of the church in kingdom warfare? What power does Satan and his demons have over the human race? What are Satan's tactics and weapons of war? What authority does the church have to fight in this "cosmic war?" What can Satan and his demons do to true believers? Can Christians be demonized? What power does Satan and his demons have over churches? Can demonic forces work their way into positions of power and influence in churches so as to hinder their work and stop the moving of the Holy Spirit and the flow of spiritual gifts? Do demonic forces operate in regional principalities and powers? Does the church have authority to displace them?

By and large, these questions have not been adequately answered by the Western church; leaving her very vulnerable and powerless in the face of satanic assault. The churches in Argentina, Korea and China have led the way in the bringing new awareness to these issues over the last twenty years. They have demonstrated the power and the authority the church of Jesus Christ has against the kingdom of darkness, thereby providing the Western church new insight into *unveiling the mask of darkness.*

The Strategy, The Battlefields

and the Weapons of Darkness

My Dear Wormwood,

Obviously you are making excellent progress. My only fear is, lest in attempting to hurry the patient you awaken him to a sense of his real position. For you and I, who see that position as it really is, must never forget how totally different it ought to appear to him. We know that we have introduced a change of direction in his course which is already carrying him out of his orbit around the Enemy; but he must be made to imagine that all the choices which have effected this change of course are trivial and revocable. He must not be allowed to suspect that he is actually now, however slowly, heading right away from the sun on a line which will carry him into the cold dark of utmost space...

Your affectionate Uncle,

Screwtape

Lewis, The Screwtape Letters

She sat transfixed, as if frozen in mid-sentence. It was not the first time the woman had become catatonic during a counseling session. My associate and I looked at one another, wondering, but not speaking. We both knew what the other was thinking. "What power was at work in this woman?"

Each counseling session ended in the same manner. While discussing her childhood, as it related to her current life, she would become unresponsive and incoherent. When she recovered there would be no memory of having stopped the conversation for long periods of time. There were large holes in her memory of childhood and teen years. Those memories that were shared carried heavy shades of darkness and evil. She was desperately crying for help as every area of her life was out of control.

The marriage relationship was distant and abusive. The children were undisciplined and having difficulty at school. She was overweight; struggling emotionally; and spiritually inconsistent. Satan was tormenting this woman and we needed to find a way to help her.

Enemy Secrets Revealed

What great frustration it would be for a general to have his secret war plans consistently revealed to the enemy. That is exactly what was happening to the King of Aram in his war against Israel. Every time the king established his battle plan, the Lord would reveal it to his prophet. Elisha would send them to the king of Israel, so he could avoid the attack (2 Kings 6:8-23)

Enraged by this obvious act of treason, the king of Aram called his generals to a meeting. "Who is giving away our battle secrets," he stormed. "None, my lord, O King," said one of his officers, "but Elisha, the prophet who is in Israel, tells the king of Israel the words that you speak in your bedroom."[20] Spies were immediately sent to locate the prophet.

Instead of capturing the prophet, the entire army was struck with blindness, by the Lord. Elisha led the enemy troops to the City of Samaria and turned them over to the king of Israel. While the army of Aram was standing before the king of Israel, the prophet prayed and their eyes were opened. They had been defeated by the prophet of God, yet again. Elisha instructed the king of Israel to feed the army of Aram then send them back to their king. This was done and the war between Israel and Aram was ended; defeated by the prophet of God, yet again. Elisha instructed the king of Israel to feed the army of Aram then send them back to their king. This was done and the war between Israel and Aram was ended.

Almighty God has done a similar thing to the kingdom of darkness. The Apostle Paul wrote to the church at Corinth, regarding the man who had been disciplined by the church for moral failure, "For to this end I also wrote, that I might put you to the test, whether you are obedient in all things. Lest Satan should take advantage of us; for we are not ignorant of his devices."[21]

God has not left His church or His children defenseless before the kingdom of darkness. He knows every scheme and evil plan the enemy prepares in the secret chambers of hell. God will reveal those plans to His faithful ones and give instructions for victory. They must be willing to wait on the Lord and ask for wisdom and divine strategy to be victorious over every attack of Satan.

Waiting on the Lord for revelation of the enemy's secret weapons and to receive divine strategy will not happen, if the church believes these things to be mere fables and fantasies. The issue will not even come up. The idea will not enter their thoughts, since such things are not real, according to their world view.

But, the demonic realm is real! The Lord Jesus Christ and the Apostles knew

that to be so and gave important instructions regarding their *modus operandi.*
The Apostle Paul wrote these instructions to the church at Ephesus.

> *Finally, my brethren, be strong in the Lord, and in the power of*
> *His might. Put on the whole armor of God, that ye may be able to*
> *stand against the wiles of the devil. For we wrestle not against flesh*
> *and blood, but against principalities, against powers, against the*
> *rulers of the darkness of this world, against spiritual wickedness in*
> *high places. Wherefore take unto you the whole armor of God, that*
> *ye may be able to withstand in the evil day, and having done all, to*
> *stand.*[22]

Jesus gave insight into the enemy's objectives when He said, "The thief does
not come except to steal, and to kill, and to destroy. I have come that they
may have life, and that they may have it more abundantly."[23] Every attack of
the enemy has the purpose of stealing, killing and destroying the child of
God. He wants to steal their joy, peace, hope and love. He seeks to kill their
sense of worth, self-acceptance, and destiny. He will try to destroy their mind,
will, emotions and physical body.

Satan's ultimate goal is to destroy Jesus Christ and the kingdom of God; then
establish himself upon the throne to be worshipped as deity.

> *He is the super-godfather with some long-standing goals which he is*
> *determined to achieve at any cost. He keeps his vast array of troops*
> *mobilized; he has a program.*

> *The devil's objectives are based in his sworn enmity against Jesus*
> *Christ. Back in the Garden of Eden, when Eve hurtled the human*

race into rebellion against the Creator, God answered Satan's
declaration of war. "From now on," he declared. "You and the
woman will be enemies, as will all of your offspring and hers. He
[Jesus Christ] shall strike you on your head, while you will strike at
his heel" (Gen. 3:15). The die has been cast. It was Satan the
Enemy versus Christ the Redeemer.[24]

Satan knows he must destroy mankind if he is to reach his ultimate goal. He seeks to accomplish this lofty goal by encouraging continued rebellion against the authority and rule of God. This can be seen in the devil's accusation against Job, before Almighty God. "Now there was a day when the sons of God came to present themselves before the LORD, and Satan also came among them. And the LORD said to Satan, 'From where do you come?' So Satan answered the LORD and said,' From going to and fro on the earth, and from walking back and forth on it.' Then the LORD said to Satan, 'Have you considered My Servant Job, that there is none like him on the earth, a blameless and upright man, one who fears God and shuns evil?' So Satan answered the LORD and said, '"Does Job fear God for nothing? Have You not made a hedge around him, around his household, and around all that he has on every side? You have blessed the work of his hands, and his possessions have increased in the land. But now, stretch out Your hand and touch all that he has, *and he will surely curse You to Your face!'* (emphasis mine)[25]

"Again there was a day when the sons of God came to present themselves before the LORD, and Satan came also among them to present himself before the LORD. And the LORD said to Satan, 'From where do you come?' So Satan answered the LORD and said, "From going to and fro on the earth, and from walking back and forth on it." Then the LORD said to Satan, 'Have you considered My Servant Job, that there is none like him on the earth, a blameless and upright man, one who fears God and shuns evil? And still he holds fast to his integrity, although you incited Me against him, to destroy him without cause.' So Satan answered the LORD and said, 'Skin for skin! Yes, all that a man has he will give for his life. But stretch out Your hand now, and touch his bone and his flesh, and *he will surely curse You to Your face!* (emphasis mine)[26]

Satan fulfills his purposes with the most cruel and diabolical methods and tools. There is no match for him, on the human plane, when it comes to evil schemes and planning the destruction of human life. One of the seven things God hates is "a heart that devises wicked plans."[27] Who can withstand the onslaught of hell's belligerence? How does a person fight against these forces of darkness?

It is important to remember God's covenant with mankind is still in effect. Genesis 3:15 provides the victorious redemptive work that restores the sons of Adam to their covenant position as steward of all creation. "For He delivered us from the domain of darkness, and transferred us to the kingdom of His Beloved Son, in whom we have redemption, the forgiveness of sins."[28] It is still God's plan for mankind "to be fruitful; to multiply; to replenish the earth; subdue it; take dominion over it" (Genesis 1:28 KJV). Therefore, every human being is the target for Satan's destructive work. A three prong attack has been established against the human race and the kingdom of God.

> ➢ Personal attacks to steal, kill and destroy individual human lives
> ➢ Control regions, territories, neighborhoods, and cities by corrupting the governments to steal, kill and destroy human lives and to destroy the authority and rule of the kingdom of God in that area.

➢ Corrupt and control the church of Jesus Christ so as to steal, kill and destroy human lives and to destroy the authority and power of the kingdom of God.

A Diabolical Strategy to Destroy Mankind

What are the strategies and weapons used by Satan and his demons to accomplish these objectives? Four primary strategies are used by the demonic hosts. They are various levels of demonic attack and control over human agencies; to suppress the color and beauty of life; to remove joy and purposeful living; to hinder the influence and power of the Word of God and to prevent the establishment of the kingdom of God in human hearts and human agencies.

These four levels are progressive in nature, leading from one level to the next, until the kingdom of darkness gains ownership of that person, territory or government. Once ownership has been established by the kingdom of darkness, they will use that individual, territory or government as their agent of darkness to oppress human lives and to war against the kingdom of God. Demonic ownership of a human life means living out of control, torture of the mind, emotions and physical body; and eventual damnation for eternity in the Lake of Fire (Revelation 20:15). For territories, cities and neighborhoods, demonic ownership means oppressive spiritual darkness, societal decay, corruption, vice and violence of every kind will fill the area. Demonic ownership of governments will bring the oppressive and destructive rule of a Nero, Adolph Hitler, or Idi Amin.

The research conducted by George Otis, Jr. gives interesting insight into the demonic strategies against people groups, territories and governments. He entitles it, "A Common Pain: From Traumas to Pact."

> *The experiences of Babel's outbound tribes were as varied as their tongues and destinations. But a careful examination of history reveals at least one important common denominator: At one point or another along their long march, each of these ancient peoples encountered some form of collective trauma.*
>
> *Regardless of whether Satan caused these circumstances or simply took advantage of them, their effect was to provide him a direct entree into the psyches of otherwise distracted people. It was a perfect setup. Not only did the trauma provoke open discussion of supernatural powers; it also prompted distraught souls to call on these powers.*
>
> *By posing as golden age deities capable of delivering the community from their present ordeal, demonic agents lured a desperate general populace into long-term quid pro quo pacts. The deal was simple. In return for allegiance pledged to these masquerading demons, the community would receive immediate trauma relief as well as restored access to the power, wisdom and deities of their forefathers.[29]*

Five notable adversities were used by the demonic hosts to bring about the trauma and the pacts. Intimidating natural barriers, climatic and natural disasters, disease and pestilence, famine and environmental ruin, wars and raids [30]

This same strategy was used by the forces of darkness against the Children of Israel as they were about to enter the Promise Land.

> *And the LORD spake unto Moses, saying, "Send thou men, that*
> *they may search the land of Canaan, which I give unto the children*
> *of Israel: of every tribe of their fathers shall ye send a man, everyone*
> *a ruler among them."*[31]

Twelve men were sent by Moses to spy out the land and bring back a report. What type of land is it? How bountiful? What kinds of people live there? (Numbers 13:1-33) The spies were on the mission for forty days. When they returned, two men, Joshua and Caleb, declared the land should be taken immediately for it was exactly as the Lord had said, "A land flowing with milk and honey" (Exodus 3:17). The other men gave an evil report. "The land, through which we have gone to search it, is a land that eateth up the inhabitants thereof; and all the people that we saw in it are men of a great stature. And there we saw the giants, the sons of Anak, which come of the giants: and we were in our own sight as grasshoppers, and so we were in their sight."[32]

The results were disastrous to the men and women who had come out of Egypt. The Lord denied them entrance into the Promise Land and sent them back to the wilderness to live until their death. The only exceptions were Joshua and Caleb and their families (Numbers 14:20-25).

This same strategy is used on individual human beings. The enemy will send adversity, trials, enticements or other harassments, seeking to break the human will and find an entrance into their life. The objective is to oppress the person to the point that their life becomes suppressed in some measure.

Suppression is the limitation of a person's life, a community, region or national life to some degree. *Funk and Wagnall's* Standard *Encyclopedic Dictionary* (J. G. Ferguson Publishing, Chicago, 1971) defines the word *suppress* as: *"To put an end or stop to; quell; crush, as a rebellion. To stop or prohibit the activities of; also to abolish. To withhold from knowledge or publication, as a book, news, etc. To repress, as a groan or sigh."*

The enemy will seek to use those things that are common to human life such as tragedies, natural disasters, sickness or disease for his advantage in oppressing and suppressing a person. Other times he will use the powers of darkness and the sinful nature of the human heart to bring adversity, temptation, or other tragedies such as physical or sexual abuse.

The demonic goal is to suppress a person's emotions, personality, relationships, creativity, physical skills and any other area of healthy living. Once a person is sufficiently suppressed they will become fixated upon, or obsessed with that area of their life. Obsession is "to occupy or trouble the mind of; to an excessive degree; a compulsive idea or emotion persistently coming to awareness."[33] Through this fixation an enemy stronghold can be effectively established sending tormentors into other areas of the person's life.

Strongholds can also be established in neighborhoods, cities and governments through societal fixations. From these fixations the powers of darkness will begin sending out tormentors into other neighborhoods and regions. Little by little these tormentors gain more territory and establish more strongholds. With each new stronghold come a greater intimidation, domination and control of the personality and life. Left unchecked the person or territory will come under the ownership of the kingdom of darkness.

What are the Enemy's Weapons?

Effective warfare against the powers of darkness not only requires understanding the enemy's strategy; it is equally important to know his weaponry, method of attack; and a working knowledge of the battlefield. No army commander would lead his men into battle without this critical information. The Scriptures give important insight into these matters.

> *Let no man say when he is tempted, I am tempted of God: for God cannot be tempted with evil, neither tempteth he any man. But every man is tempted, when he is drawn away of his own lust, and enticed. Then when lust hath conceived, it bringeth forth sin: and sin, when it is finished, bringeth forth death. Do not err, my beloved brethren.[34]*

Satan's plan of attack is quite simple. The enemy learns the inherent weakness found in every person, culture and government then exploits them. Mankind's vulnerability to these attacks comes from the sin nature spoken of by King David in the Psalms and referred to by the Apostle Paul.

> *Behold, I was brought forth in iniquity, And in sin my mother conceived me.[35]*

> *Therefore, just as through one man sin entered into the world, and death through sin, and so death spread to all men, because all sinned.[36]*

41

God knows the hearts of men. *"I, the LORD your God, am a jealous God, visiting the iniquity of the fathers on the children, on the third and the fourth generations of those who hate Me, but showing loving kindness to thousands, to those who love Me and keep My commandments."*[37] He repeated this truth to Moses on the mountain, when the glory of God was revealed to him.

> *Then the LORD passed by in front of him and proclaimed, 'The LORD, the LORD God, compassionate and gracious, slow to anger, and abounding in lovingkindness and truth; who keeps lovingkindness for thousands, who forgives iniquity, transgression and sin; yet He will by no means leave the guilty unpunished, visiting the iniquity of fathers on the children and on the grandchildren to the third and fourth generations.*[38]

This truth is self-evident when a parent is raising children. Left to himself, a child will be selfish, spoiled, deceptive and ungrateful. Parents must diligently train their children to tell the truth and not to lie; to share their toys and not be selfish; to be obedient and not be self-willed; to be respectful, kind, use good manners not be temperamental, hateful and crude; to be honest and not to steal. These character qualities do not just happen. Discipline and training must be intentional and purposeful if a child is to grow up trustworthy, dependable, sincere and kind.

An Issue of Mankind's Spiritual DNA

The humanistic, rationalistic and materialistic world view of the Western culture does not allow for such a concept of mankind. They have adopted the presupposition man is basically good.

> *Among the most fundamental Freudian ideas is the notion that*
> *human behavior, and consequently the direction that personality*
> *development takes, derives from two powerful tendencies: the human*
> *urge to survive and the urge to procreate. The new born infant has a*
> *simple, undeveloped personality, consisting solely of the primitive*
> *urges (Eros and Thanatos) that will be a lifetime source of psychic*
> *energy.39*

Dr. Jay Adams addressed this issue in his book, Competent to Counsel.

> *Roger's fundamental denial of man's sinful nature. He wrote: 'One*
> *of the most revolutionary concepts to grow out of our clinical*
> *experience is the growing recognition that the innermost core of*
> *man's nature, the deepest levels of his personality, the base of his*
> *'animal nature' is positive in character - is basically socialized,*
> *forward-moving, rational and realistic.'40*

These concepts have also crept into the church, weakening her resolve and making her ineffective in the fight against the powers of darkness. Most Christian counseling is based upon the presuppositions of atheistic men, such as Sigmund Freud, Carl Rogers, or William Glasser. These are men who deny the authority of Scripture; Divine creation of the human race; and the sinful nature mankind. The medical model has replaced the principle of sinful behavior making alcoholism, drug addiction, or abusive behavior a sickness that needs to be treated with twelve step programs, rather than a sin that needs to be repented of and cleansed by God. Sermons against sin have been softened and in some cases even replaced by teachings in psychology, behavior modification and self-improvement.

Acceptance of humanistic ideology by the church has left the Western culture vulnerable to the worst attacks of hell. Satan has been able to establish great strongholds in nations that were once bastions of truth and light.

Two generations of American children have grown up without quality discipline and training in manners, character and right behavior. Parents have believed the lie about children being basically good. Schools have diligently taught the children to question authority. The disastrous results are revealed in the research of William J. Bennett, former drug czar and Secretary of Education.

> *Since 1960, violent crime has shot up 560 percent; illegitimate births increased 400%; quadrupling of divorce rates; tripling of percentage of young people in single parent homes; 200% increase in teenage suicide rate and drop of 754 points in the average SAT score. "The United States ranks near the top of the industrialized world in rates of abortion, divorce and unwed births. We lead the industrialized world in murder, rape, and violent crime. In elementary and secondary education, we are at or near the bottom in achievement scores. These outward manifestations - and our complacency about them - are signs of a deeper decay; one that doesn't lend itself so easily to quantitative analysis. There is a coarseness, a callousness, a cynicism, a banality and vulgarity to our time. There are too many signs of a civilization gone rotten. The worst of it has to do with our children: We live in a culture that at times almost seems dedicated to the corruption of the young. The real*

crisis of our times is spiritual. The ancients called it "acedia" - the
spiritual sloth or deadening, an undue concern to external affairs
and an absence of zeal for divine things. It eventually leads to a
hatred of the good altogether. Only when we turn our affections and
desires toward the right things - toward enduring, noble, spiritual
things - will our problems get better.[41]

The church must return to the truth. Every child is uniquely created by Almighty God according to His blue print, with purpose and destiny. "For thou hast possessed my reins: thou hast covered me in my mother's womb. I will praise thee; for I am fearfully and wonderfully made: marvelous are thy works; and that my soul knoweth right well. My substance was not hid from thee, when I was made in secret, and curiously wrought in the lowest parts of the earth. Thine eyes did see my substance, yet being imperfect; and in thy book all my members were written, which in continuance were fashioned, when as yet there was none of them."[42]

Every child also has a distinct weakness. This weakness comes from the generational DNA that not only determines physical characteristics that are unique to the family; but also emotional, personality, relational, behavioral and spiritual weaknesses that are passed from generation to generation. It is the iniquity of the fathers being visited to the third and fourth generations. It is each child being conceived in sin and shaped in iniquity from their mother's womb (Ps. 51:5). It is the solidarity mankind has with their original parents, Adam and Eve.

It is the same with regions, territories and governments. There are those traits that are common to certain cultures such as the stoic Italian, English stiff

45

upper lip, Irish temper, and French sensuality, hot blood German and every other nationality and culture of the world. These characteristics are passed from generation to generation through the cultural and social DNA of that region, territory or nation. The Apostle Paul gave an insightful description of the enemy's battlefield and plan of action in his epistle to the church at Ephesus.

> *And you were dead in your trespasses and sins, in which you*
> *formerly walked according to the course of this world, according to*
> *the prince of the power of the air, of the spirit that is now working*
> *in the sons of disobedience. Among them we too all formerly lived in*
> *the lusts of our flesh, indulging the desires of the flesh and of the*
> *mind, and were by nature children of wrath, even as the rest.*[43]

It is important to notice; mankind is "by nature children of wrath." We are not basically good and bent toward right. Mankind is by nature sinful and bent toward wrong.

The enemy will seek to exploit these weaknesses by attacking the mind, will, emotions or natural appetites of the flesh with adversity or enticements. The individual or populace must choose whether to yield to the enticement or adversity and surrender their members to sinful behavior or whether they will resist and obey God. Rarely, do they immediately understand the painful cost of yielding to the enemy's strategy. The enemy's plan is to make death appear as life. The serpent did not show Adam and Eve the murder scene of their son, when he tempted them to eat of the forbidden tree. He told them they would be like God (Genesis 3:4-5). The old saying is very true.

46

Sin will always cost you more than you intended to pay;
Take you farther than you intended to stray,
Keep you longer than you intended to stay.

The Enemy's Arsenal

The powers of darkness will use a variety of methods to oppress man's basic nature seeking to gain a foothold of intimidation, domination and control. There are seven mighty weapons he primarily uses in his arsenal.

Pride

The kingdom of darkness was birthed in the pride that filled Satan's heart (Isaiah 14:12-18). Satan's arrogance had its roots in his physical beauty (Ezekiel 28:12-18). The original sin took place in the Garden of Eden, as a result of the serpent's appeal to the pride of Adam and Eve (Genesis 3:1-7). Pride is one of the three root sins of mankind. "For all that is in the world, the lust of the flesh, and the lust of the eyes, and the pride of life, is not of the Father, but is of the world."[44] Satan will use pride to keep people from seeking God (Psalm 10:4). Jesus said pride comes out of the heart of a person and defiles them (Mark 7:22). Pride is the root of all contention and strife (Proverbs 13:10). The Apostle John wrote of the dangers pride and how Satan will use it to fight against the church. "I wrote unto the church: but Diotrephes, who loveth to have the preeminence among them, receiveth us not. Wherefore, if I come, I will remember his deeds which he doeth, prating against us with malicious words: and not content therewith, neither doth he himself receive the brethren, and forbiddeth them that would, and casteth them out of the church. Beloved, follow not that which is evil, but that which is good. He that doeth good is of God: but he that doeth evil hath not seen God."[45]

"Pride goeth before destruction and a haughty spirit before a fall" (Proverbs 16:18 KJV).

Greed

Satan's heart is not only filled with pride, but with greed.

> *'You were the anointed cherub who covers, and I placed you*
> *{there.} You were on the holy mountain of God; you walked in the*
> *midst of the stones of fire. You were blameless in your ways from the*
> *day you were created, until unrighteousness was found in you. By the*
> *abundance of your trade you were internally filled with violence, and*
> *you sinned; there-fore I have cast you as profane from the mountain*
> *of God. And I have destroyed you, O covering cherub, from the*
> *midst of the stones of fire.'[46]*

Satan tempted Balaam to prophesy against the people of God for great wealth (Numbers 22-23). The Apostle Peter warned the church in 2 Peter 2:1-16 of the demonic strategies used against Balaam. Jude warned of these same strategies in Jude 1-11. Jesus also warned the Church at Pergamos of these satanic strategies (Revelation 2:14). The Apostle Paul wrote to Timothy that the love of money is the root of all evil. He gave five dangers of greed in 1 Timothy 6:9-10. It makes a person more vulnerable to temptation, it sets a spiritual snare, it creates foolish and hurtful lusts which will drown a person in destruction and perdition, it causes a person to err from the faith, and it pierces a person through with many sorrows.

Jericho was the tithe city of the Promise Land, set apart by God. No one was to take spoil for themselves, it was all to go into the treasury of the Lord (Joshua 6:17-19). One greedy man took some of the spoil bringing judgment upon himself, his family and the nation of Israel (Joshua 7:1-21). Ananias and Sapphira lied to the Holy Spirit when they told the Apostle Peter in Acts 5:1-10 that they were bringing the whole price of their land as an offering to God. They kept part of the money for themselves, lying to the Holy Spirit and the Apostles. Judgment was both swift and deadly.

Appetites of the Flesh

Demonic forces corrupted the early generations of mankind through sexual sins (Genesis 6:1-5). Satan trapped the Israelites by tempting them with sexual sins in Numbers 25:1-8 and 31:16. Satan took down Samson in Judges 16:5-20 by enticing him through the appetites of the flesh. The Apostle Paul warned the church at Thessalonica of this powerful weapon of the enemy (1 Thessalonians 4:1-8), and also warned his spiritual son, Timothy, of the strong snare these appetites are to men of God who want to be vessels of honor in the house of the Lord in 2 Timothy 2:19-26.

Rebellion and Stubbornness

Satan is the author of rebellion. He planned an attempted overthrow of heaven as described in Isaiah 14:13-15. He prompted a rebellion against Moses and Aaron by Korah and Dathan in Numbers 16:1-50. Saul was a self-willed and rebellious king over Israel, animated by powers of darkness (1

49

Samuel 13:1-14; 15:1-11). We read in 1 Samuel 15:23 that rebellion is like witchcraft and stubbornness is like iniquity and idolatry. The Apostle Paul warned the church in 2 Timothy 2:23-3:9 of the dangers of rebellion and stubbornness.

Bitterness

Unforgiveness gives the enemy a foothold (Ephesians 4:26-27). "Give place to the devil" in Ephesians 4:27 means to give him an area of jurisdiction. Jesus declared in Matthew 18:21-25 that unforgiveness in a person's heart causes God to have to turn you over to tormentors. Bitterness will bring defiling into every area of a person's life, relationships, and endeavor (Hebrews12:14-16).

Condemnation

Satan was the accuser against Job (Job 1:1-12; 2:1-7). He is called "the accuser of the brethren" in Revelation 12:10 and accuses the believer to God day and night. The tactics he uses are domination, intimidation and control. The Midianites used these tactics to keep Israel in bondage to their tyrannical rule in Judges 6:1-5. In 1 Samuel 17:1-24 we read that the Philistines used this same tactic against Israel with Goliath. The enemy has used this mighty weapon to control people, groups, and nations for centuries. The following are some examples of the means used by the enemy in history.

The Assyrians "depended upon frightfulness as a means of overcoming their enemies. Upon soldiers captured in battle, and some upon noncombatants as well, they inflicted unspeakable cruelties such as, skinning them alive, impaling them on stakes, cutting off ears, noses and sex organs, and then exhibiting the mutilated victims in cages for the benefit of cities that had not yet surrendered. The accounts of these cruelties come from the records of the Assyrians themselves. Their chronicles boasted of them as evidence of their valor"[47]

The Roman Empire used crucifixion and other means of cruelty to intimidate their subjects. "'In so much that (as Eusebius recordeth) one might then see cities full of men's bodies, the old there lying together with the young, and the dead bodies of women cast out naked, without all reverence of that sex in the open streets.'"[48]

The Nazi's used open cruelty to bring intimidation, domination and control. "The prisoners then recalled scraps of information so nightmarish that it could hardly be believed. They went back to the period just after the end of World War I, when the name of Corporal Adolph Hitler had begun to appear. . . his storm troops (SA), the main purpose of which was to spread terror. . . demonstrations occurred in Berlin in 1932. . . *Reich Stag* was set on fire. . ... Unused factories were changed into the first concentration camps. The Nazis had put thousands of Germans behind wires and bars. 250,000 anti-fascists were sent to concentration camps up till 1939, and 32,000 among them were executed with the ax."[49] [In the early years it was not just Jews who were placed in concentration camps. Germans, who were believed to be anti-Nazi, were also interned.]

The powers of darkness have used dominating fathers or mothers, employers, husbands, boyfriends and other family members to inflict his damage and gain a foothold in individual lives. Intimidation, domination and control are maintained through mental and emotional abuse, physical abuse, sexual abuse

51

Satanic Ritual Abuse (SRA), jealousy, anger and temper.

Whether attacking a small child or seeking to gain control over a whole nation, these seven weapons have proved very effective for the powers of darkness. Satan and his demonic army use them with skill and deadly intent. God has not left the human race vulnerable to these forces, without protection and hope of victory. He has given to us weapons that are "mighty, through God, to the pulling down of strongholds."[50]

A Crushing Defeat

My Dear Wormwood,

I have been thinking very hard about the question in your last letter. If, as I have clearly shown, all selves are by their very nature in competition, and therefore the Enemy's idea of Love is a contradiction in terms, what becomes of my reiterated warning that He really loves the human vermin and really desires their freedom and continued existence? The truth is, I slipped by mere carelessness into saying that the Enemy really loves the humans. That, of course, is an impossibility. He is one being, they are distinct from Him. Their good cannot be His. All His talk about Love must be a disguise for something else - He must have some <u>real</u> motive for creating them and taking so much trouble about them. The reason one comes to talk as If He really had this impossible Love is our utter failure to find out that real motive. What does He stand to make out of them? That is the insoluble question. I do not see that it can do any harm to tell you that this very problem was a chief cause of Our Father's quarrel with the Enemy. When the creation of man was first mooted and when, even at That Stage, the Enemy freely confessed that he fore-saw a certain episode about a cross, Our Father very naturally sought an interview and asked for an explanation. The Enemy gave no reply except to produce the cock-and-bull story about disinterested Love which He has been circulating ever since. This Our Father naturally could not accept. He implored the Enemy to lay His cards on the table, and give Him every opportunity. He admitted that he felt real anxiety to know the secret; the Enemy replied, 'I wish with all my heart that you did." It was, I imagine, at this stage in the interview that Our Father's disgust at such an unprovoked lack of confidence caused him to remove himself an infinite distance from the Presence with a suddenness which has given rise to the ridiculous Enemy story that he was forcibly thrown out of Heaven.

Your affectionate uncle,
Screwtape
Lewis, The Screwtape Letters

"I will not let her go!" screamed the demonic spirit, as he controlled the counseling session with the woman for about an hour, as this force of darkness began to manifest. We had recognized signs of significant spiritual problems as the counseling session had progressed through the various relationship issues for which she was seeking help. These spiritual issues had to be resolved if she was to see a change in her relationship relationships. The counseling had been directed in that manner. We discussed various scriptural principles regarding relationships and asked permission to pray for her about those spiritual issues. She very much wanted prayer. It was during this time of prayer the demonic spirit manifested itself, challenging our authority to lead the woman to freedom. New questions needed to be addressed. How had this demon and his companions come into the woman's life? What gave them the right to hold her captive? What would be the best approach for setting her free? Exactly what authority did we have to set her free?

The "Seed of Woman" Comes on the Scene

Mankind's ability to stand against the forces of darkness is not resident within himself. The Psalmist declared, "Through God we shall do valiantly: for He it is that shall tread down our enemies."[51] King David wrote:

> *Lift up your heads, O you gates; be lifted up, you ancient doors,*
> *that the King of glory may come in. Who is this King of glory? The*
> *LORD strong and mighty, the LORD mighty in battle. Lift up*

your heads, O you gates; lift them up, you ancient doors, that the
King of glory may come in. Who is he, this King of glory? The
LORD Almighty he is the King of glory.

While mankind was still in the Garden of Eden, God declared defeat to the serpent and the evil powers of darkness. "And I will put enmity between you and the woman, and between your seed and her seed; He shall bruise you on the head, and you shall bruise him on the heel" (Genesis 3:15). That day came at the most unexpected time; in the most unexpected place; and by the most unexpected person.

Jesus had been away from His hometown, Nazareth, for several weeks. Upon His return, He went to the synagogue on the Sabbath day and was asked to read the Scriptures. He opened the scroll to the Book of Isaiah and read.

The Spirit of the Lord is upon Me, Because He anointed Me to
preach the gospel to the poor. He has sent Me to proclaim release to
the captives, And recovery of sight to the blind, To set free those who
are downtrodden, To proclaim the favorable year of the Lord.[52]

He then sat down and said, "Today this Scripture has been fulfilled in your hearing" (Luke 4:21). The people could hardly believe what they were hearing. This was Joseph and Mary's son. He had grown up in their community. What was He saying? Was He declaring himself to be the Messiah? Had He gone mad while He was away? They wanted to stone Him for these blasphemous statements, but He was able to get away.

Jesus was, indeed, declaring Himself to be the Messiah; and even more. He

55

was proclaiming Himself to be the "Seed of Woman." The long awaited day for mankind's deliverance had arrived, at last.

An Attempt to Destroy the "Seed of Woman"

God told Abraham that his descendants would serve as slaves in Egypt for four hundred years (Genesis 15:13). This was fulfilled when Joseph became governor of Egypt and moved his father and brothers' families there, so they could escape the famine in their home land (Genesis 45:1-15). Joseph had great favor with the Pharaoh. His father and family were granted royal honor and given the Land of Goshen in which to settle (Genesis 45:16-20; 47:1-6).

Following the death of Joseph, the powers of darkness enraged the new Pharaoh and the Egyptians against the Israelites. It was a calculated move on the part of Satan to destroy God's people and to stop the "Seed of Woman" from being born. Satan inspired Pharaoh and his people to enslave the Israelites and to kill all of the male children born into Hebrew families.

Now there arose a new king over Egypt, who did not know Joseph. And he said to his people, 'Look, the people of the children of Israel are more and mightier than we; come, let us deal shrewdly with them, lest they multiply, and it happen, in the event of war, that they also join our enemies and fight against us, and so go up out of the land.'

Therefore, they set taskmasters over them to afflict them with their burdens. And they built for Pharaoh supply cities, Pithom and Rameses. But the more they afflicted them, the more they multiplied and grew. And they were in dread of the children of Israel. So the Egyptians made the children of Israel serve with rigor.

Then the king of Egypt spoke to the Hebrew midwives, of whom the name of one was Shiphrah and the name of the other Puah; and he said, 'When you do the duties of a midwife for the Hebrew women, and see them on the birthstools, if it is a son, then you shall kill him; but if it is a daughter, then she shall live.'[53]

After four hundred and thirty years, God heard the cry of His people and called Moses to deliver them from Egyptian slavery (Ex. 12:40-41).

'Therefore say to the children of Israel: "I am the LORD; I will bring you out from under the burdens of the Egyptians, I will rescue you from their bondage, and I will redeem you with an outstretched arm and with great judgments. I will take you as My people, and I will be your God. Then you shall know that I am the LORD your God who brings you out from under the burdens of the Egyptians. And I will bring you into the land which I swore to give to Abraham, Isaac, and Jacob; and I will give it to you as a heritage: I am the LORD.'" [54]

Human agency would not deliver the people. God, Himself, would release the captive, "with an outstretched arm and with mighty acts of judgment." Moses would be God's ambassador to Pharaoh, speaking God's message and bringing signs and wonders. The power and the authority by which Moses did the work would be God's

57

mighty arm.

*The message to Pharaoh was simple. "Let my people go, so that
they may worship Me" (Exodus 8:1). If he refused, God would
send judgment against the land. Ten times Moses confronted
Pharaoh with the message. Ten times God had to send plagues,
because Pharaoh hardened his heart against the word of the Lord.
Each encounter was a confrontation between Almighty God and the
prophets, sorcerers and magicians of Egypt's false gods (Exodus
7:11, 22; 8:7, 18; 9:11). God "made a mockery of the
Egyptians" and revealed His glory and mighty power for all the
world to see (Exodus 10:2).*

*When God turned Moses' staff into a serpent, the false gods
duplicated the act. When God turned the water to blood and sent
frogs on the land, the false gods performed the same miracles. When
God sent swarming gnats over the land, "The magicians tried with
their secret arts to bring forth gnats, but they could not. Then the
magicians said to Pharaoh, 'This is the finger of God.'"[55] When
God sent boils upon man and beast, the magicians could not stand
before Moses, for they were also plagued with the boils. Each plague
sent by God was a direct judgment against the false deities of Egypt.
The Nile River and all of the water of the land became blood
(Exodus 7:19), the land was covered with frogs (Exodus 8:5-6),
lice (gnats) came out of the dust in the land of Egypt (Exodus
8:16-17), great swarms of flies covered the nation (Exodus 8:24),
Egyptian cattle were plagued (Exodus 9:6), boils came on the
bodies of the Egyptians and their animals (Exodus 9:10), severe
hail and lightning storms came on the land (Exodus 9:24), locust*

58

swarms ate all vegetation in Egypt (Exodus 10:14-15), complete
darkness covered the land of Egypt for three days (Exodus10:22),
and death came to the first born in all of the families and animals
of Egypt (Exodus 12:12).

God's judgment was not only against Pharaoh and the Egyptians, He was judging the authority of Satan and the kingdom of darkness manifested through the prophets, sorcerers and magicians of Egypt (Exodus 12:12).

"I Will Redeem You"

The last plague was the definitive redeeming work that would release Israel from slavery. "And all the first-born in the land of Egypt shall die, from the first-born of Pharaoh who sits on the throne, even to the first-born of the slave girl who is behind the millstones; all the first-born of the cattle as well."[56]

While the death angel was moving over the land of Egypt taking the life of every first born, the Israelites would be protected from death and delivered from Egyptian slavery by the blood of a sacrificed lamb.

God said, "I will bring you out from under the burdens of the Egyptians, and I will redeem you with an outstretched arm and with great judgments."[57] Detailed instructions were to be followed by the Israelites for this special night of God's deliverance.

On the tenth day of Abib they were to select a male lamb or goat, one-year-old, who was without blemish (Exodus 12:1-2, 5; 13:4). Each household was to select a lamb. If the family was too small to eat a lamb, they were to join with another family and select a lamb for the two families to sacrifice and eat (Exodus 12:3). On the fourteenth day of the month the animal was to be butchered (Exodus 12:6) and the blood was to be caught in a basin and painted onto the door posts of the house in which the meal would be eaten (Exodus 12:7). The lamb was to be roasted (not boiled nor eaten raw); and eaten that same night with bitter herbs and unleavened bread (Exodus 12:8-9). It was to be eaten in its entirety before dawn. Any of the meat remaining at dawn was to be burned in the fire (Exodus 12:10). The people were to eat the meal dressed in their traveling clothes, packed and ready to leave Egypt (Exodus 12:11).

Every family who followed these instructions and had the door post of their house painted with the blood of the Passover lamb would be delivered from the death angel and released from the captivity of Egypt. Every home without the blood of the lamb, even if it was Israelite, suffered death (Exodus 12:29-32, 50-51).

The next morning, following the visitation of the death angel, the whole land of Egypt was in mourning; even Pharaoh's home had suffered the death of the first born. The land of Goshen, however, was filled with celebration and preparation for travel. Two further instructions, of great importance, had been given the Israelites regarding their day of deliverance.

They were to ask their Egyptian neighbors for their silver and gold. Grieving the loss of their first born children the Egyptian's gladly complied. Gold, silver and precious clothes were given in abundance as they begged Israel to leave their land. In this way, Israel plundered their enemy (Exodus 12:33-36).

The second instruction required Israel to establish a feast for fourteen days in the month of Abib (Nisan) to annually celebrate the remembrance of Passover for all generations (Exodus 12:14-20; 13:4-16).

One Greater Than Moses Celebrates Passover

"With *fervent* desire, I have desired to eat this meal with you," Jesus said, as he reclined to eat the Passover meal with His disciples (Luke 22:15). It was the night of His betrayal. The next day, He would face trial, be flogged and then be crucified on the cross.

John the Baptist had declared Jesus' true identity three and half years earlier. "Behold! The Lamb of God who takes away the sin of the world!"[58] As Jesus celebrated the Passover Seder, to which He had so fervently looked forward, the mystery of the first Passover, held in Egypt, was unveiled.

> *And as they were eating, Jesus took bread, blessed and broke it,*
> *and gave it to the disciples and said, "Take, eat; this is My body."*
> *Then He took the cup, and gave thanks, and gave it to them,*
> *saying, "Drink from it, all of you. For this is My blood of the new*
> *covenant, which is shed for many for the remission of sins.*[59]

Jesus Christ was the perfect Lamb of God to be sacrificed at Passover. His blood would redeem mankind from slavery to Satan, the kingdom of darkness and sin.

Satan's Attempt to Destroy the Perfect "Seed of Woman"

Satan had enraged the Roman Empire against the Israelites. He sought once more to destroy God's people and the 'Seed of Woman." This time he inspired Herod the Great to carry out his diabolical plan. King Herod was an Idumaean, a racially mixed Jew. He had conspired, murdered, and bribed his way to power, and then convinced Caesar Augustus to appoint him as King of the Jews.

At first glance, at the accomplishments of Herod the Great might cause one to think him religious. He had, after all, built the greatest Jewish temple since King Solomon. Over four hundred synagogues dotted the nation under his leadership. The priesthood of Israel and the counsel of the Sanhedrin were allowed to function, despite Roman domination and its idolatrous demands. A closer look, however, reveals these deeds were mere trappings; the proverbial smoke and mirror. The true heart of this man was pure evil.

Herod corrupted the land of Israel; much like the days of Eli and his contemptible sons, when the glory of God had departed from the land (1 Samuel 2-3).

> *Everywhere was his mark. Temples to the gods and to Caesar,*
> *magnificent, and magnificently adorned. The theater and*
> *amphitheater spoke of his Grecianism; Antonia was the*
> *representative fortress. Nor could his apparent work for the God of*
> *Israel have deceived the most credulous. Not once, not twice, but six*
> *times did he change the High-Priesthood, to bestow it at last on one*
> *who bears no good name in Jewish theology, a foreigner in Judaea,*
> *and Alexandrian.*

Herod not only corrupted the priesthood and the Jewish culture, he tried to destroy the "Seed of Woman."

When word arrived to King Herod about the Magi seeking "He who has been born King of the Jews," the demonic spirits immediately took charge. "Where [is] the Christ to be born?" Herod asked his spiritual leaders? "Bethlehem of Judea," they replied. Herod used his most cunning and oily words to implore the visitors from the East.

> *Go and make careful search for the Child; and when you have found {Him,} report to me, that I too may come and worship Him*[60]

The motive was not worship, but destruction. When the Magi did not return to him because they had been warned by an angel, Herod's rage knew no boundaries. He ordered every male child two years and younger, living in Bethlehem, to be slaughtered (Matthew 2:12-16). Like Moses, born in Egypt, Jesus was divinely protected from Satan's attempt to destroy God's promised deliverer. His parents ferreted the child out of Israel into Egypt until King Herod was no longer on the throne.

A Bruised Heel and a Crushed Head

Jesus Christ is the promised "Seed of Woman;" born in Bethlehem to the virgin Mary and her husband Joseph (Luke 1:26-36; 2:4-20; Matthew 2:1). He came into the world for the express purpose of fulfilling Genesis 3:15.

For this purpose, the Son of God was manifested, that he might
destroy the works of the devil.[61]

Just as the death of the first born in Egypt and the blood of the Passover Lamb crushed the power of Pharaoh and plundered the wealth of Egypt; the death of Jesus Christ, "the first born of all creation,"[62] and the blood of the "Lamb of God"[63] crushed the power of Satan and plundered the kingdom of darkness. At every turn of His ministry, Jesus Christ confronted the demonic powers in a way that had never been done in history.

His first encounter was a face-to-face battle with the devil, following His baptism in the Jordan River. "Then Jesus was led up of the Spirit into the wilderness to be tempted of the devil."[64] This was a reenactment of the encounter between Adam and Eve and the serpent in the Garden of Eden. This confrontation did not take place in a garden but in the desert of the Judean wilderness. This tempter was not a cunning serpent but Satan, himself. This Adam was no ordinary man, but the "Last Adam" in whom dwelt "all the fullness of the Godhead, bodily" (1 Corinthians 15:45; Colossians 2:9).

> *Now we are in another world. Before Matthew is through with the*
> *story, "the tempter" is called "the devil (4:5, 8, 11) and Jesus calls*
> *him "Satan" (v. 10). We are face-to-face with spiritual warfare of*
> *the most intense magnitude. Jesus, the Son of God meets the devil,*
> *Satan and the tempter, face-to-face in true mortal combat.*
>
> *In His public baptism, Jesus commits Himself to do the will of the*
> *Father who was already well pleased with Him (Matthew 3:13-*
> *17). In His private encounter with the tempter, He reveals that the*
> *major focus of His ministry will be against Satan, the ruler of this*

age. To win men from Satan's kingdom to God's, He must first
personally, as a man, overcome the Devil's powers.

Jesus is to be seen here as the Last Adam and the second man in
contrast to the first Adam and the first man (1 Corinthians 15:45-
47). Adam, the representative man, the Last Adam and the second
man, is to face the same temptation from the same source. Jesus was
to undo the tragedy of Adam's fall, but it was to be more difficult
for Him than it was for Adam.[65]

The first confrontation, in the Garden, involved eating fruit from the
forbidden tree and a cunning appeal to the human pride. "For God doth
know that in the day ye eat thereof, then your eyes shall be opened, and ye
shall be as gods, knowing good and evil."[66] Satan's *modus operandi* did not
change in the four thousand years between the Garden of Eden temptation
and the Judean wilderness encounter. The tempter came to him and said, "If
you are the Son of God, command that these stones to become bread...Then
the devil took Him into the Holy City; and he had Him stand on the pinnacle
of the temple. 'If you are the Son of God,' he said, 'Throw yourself
down...Again, the Devil took Him to a very high mountain and showed Him
all the kingdoms of the world and their glory. . . 'All these things will I give
you,' he said, 'If you fall down and worship me.'"[67]

What did change was the response of the man being tempted. Jesus Christ did
not yield to the cunningly crafted words from hell, even though they did
contain Scripture. He declared the truth of God's Word at every deceptive
encounter. "It is written: `Man shall not live on bread alone, but on every
word that proceeds out of the mouth of God. 'On the other hand, it is

65

written: 'You shall not put the Lord your God to the test.'" Jesus said to him, "Be gone, Satan! For it is written: `You shall worship the Lord your God, and serve Him only.'"[68]

The words of Jesus held great power and authority. It was the same kind of power and authority that God had delegated to Adam and Eve. The Last Adam refused to surrender His position of "dominion" and He "subdued" the devil with the Word of God and commanded him to leave.

> *James Morrison records Jeremy Taylor as saying that this is 'a word of indignation and of castigation and dismission. . . The Lamb of God was angry as a provoked lion, and commanded him away, when his demands were imprudent and blasphemous.' He then comments, 'The victory is achieved. The Second Adam has not fallen and will not fall.[69]*

The first blow from the "Seed of Woman" had been struck against the head of the serpent. It was a foretaste of what was to come for the next three and a half years of Jesus' ministry, as there would be continual confrontation between the Son of God and the kingdom of darkness. Luke, the evangelist adds an important postscript to the account of Jesus' wilderness temptation. "And when the devil had finished every temptation, he departs from Him until an opportune time" (Luke 4:13).

A. B. Bruce says this phrase implies that similar temptations recurred in the experience of Jesus. Geldenhuys agrees.

> *'In every possible way that he could think of he assailed the Savior, but without avail. So he departed when vanquished, but not for*

good. Again and again he renewed his attacks on Jesus on suitable occasions (cf. 11:13 and Mark 8:32-33), even though Peter.'

Geldenhuys then points to Gethsemane and the Cross as the ultimate of temptations.

> *'But it was especially when the Lord on the eve of the crucifixion wrestled in Gethsemane that Satan attacked Him. . . with all the power and savagery of hell in a desperate attempt to overcome Him before He finally triumphed in His death on the cross over all the powers of darkness and confirmed His victory through the resurrection and ascension.'[70]*

Every turn of Jesus public ministry brought an encounter with the powers of darkness.

> *Jesus declared war on Satan and his whole kingdom of demons. After all, he had come to 'destroy the works of the devil' (1 John 3:8 KJV), and from Jesus' temptation to the cross, it was an all-out, hammer-and-tongs, knock-down-drag-out battle. Satan mobilized the forces at his command, holding back no reserves. But Jesus would not give in. Every word he spoke, every deed he did, every offensive he launched was a frontal attack in his strategy to 'destroy the works of the devil.'*

> *It is noteworthy that Jesus flatly refused to demonstrate to Satan that he was indeed the Son of God by turning a stone into a loaf of bread. But when some were in honest search, he did not hesitate to let them know that he was indeed the Christ, the Son of God. For*

67

example, John the Baptist had seemed to be sure that Jesus was the
Messiah. But when he was arrested and imprisoned by Herod [son
of Herod the Great], he succumbed to despondency and began to
wonder. So, 'he sent two of his disciples to Jesus to ask him, 'are
you really the Messiah? Or shall we keep on looking for him?' The
two disciples found Jesus . . . casting out evil spirits (demons).'
When they confronted him with John's question, this was his reply:
'Go back to John and tell him all you have seen and heard here
today' (Luke 7:19-22).[71]

Jesus public confrontation with the powers of darkness was in the synagogue
at Capernaum (Mark 1:21-27). When the crowds saw his authority, they
brought even more people to him (Mark. 1:32). Matthew recorded the event.

When the even was come, they brought unto him many that were
possessed with devils: and he cast out the spirits with his word, and
healed all that were sick:[72]

Jesus cast out spirits of infirmity (Luke 13:11); deaf and dumb spirits (Mark
9:24-26; Luke 11:14); spirits that held children (Mark 7:24-30); and demons of
epilepsy (Mark 9:17-27); demons of blindness and muteness (Matthew 12:22).
"And whenever the unclean spirits beheld Him, they would fall down before
Him and cry out, saying, "You are the Son of God!"[73]

God's Greatest Demonstration of

Love

My Dear Wormwood,

You complain that my last letter does not make it clear whether I regard being in love as a desirable state for a human or not. But really, Wormwood, that is the sort of question one expects them to ask! Leave them to discuss whether" Love," or patriotism, or celibacy, or candles on altars, or teetotalism, or education, is "good" or "bad." Can't you see there's no answer? Nothing matters at all except the tendency of a given state of mind, in given circumstances, to move a particular patient at a particular moment nearer to the Enemy or nearer to us....

Your affectionate Uncle

Screwtape

Lewis, The Screwtape Letters

"It burns! It burns! It burns!" screamed the demon, as the counseling session moved from giving biblical counsel to prayer for the one who had come for help. As we prayed, the blood of Jesus Christ was declared over her. At that point, the demon began shrieking and crying out against the blood of Jesus Christ. Scripture says that is what should happen, when a demon encounters the authority and power of the blood of Jesus Christ.

And I heard a loud voice in heaven, saying, "Now the salvation,
and the power, and the kingdom of our God and the authority of
His Christ have come, for the accuser of our brethren has been
thrown down, who accuses them before our God day and night.
"And they overcame him because of the blood of the Lamb and
because of the word of their testimony, and they did not love their life
even to death. [74]

The Arrival of God's Kingdom

Four hundred years had passed since Malachi, the last prophet of Israel, proclaimed the Word of the Lord (circa 420 BC). A new prophet came preaching in the Judean wilderness, calling the people to, "Repent for the kingdom of heaven is at hand" (Matt. 3:2). The prophet Isaiah had foretold the ministry of this new and strange preacher. "The voice of one crying in the wilderness: 'Prepare the way of the LORD; Make His paths straight.'"[75] John the Baptist was to prepare the way for Jesus Christ, the "Seed of Woman," who was to come and bruise the head of the serpent. Israel and all the world was about to see the visible expression of the authority and power of God's kingdom, as it struck as decisive blow against the kingdom of darkness.

Jesus Christ came preaching the same message as John the Baptist; the kingdom of God has come among men. "From that time Jesus began to preach and to say, 'Repent, for the kingdom of heaven is at hand.'"[76] Every village, hamlet and city where Jesus went received a visible manifestation of the authority and power of God's kingdom.

And Jesus went about all Galilee, teaching in their synagogues,

preaching the gospel of the kingdom, and healing all kinds of

sickness and all kinds of disease among the people. Then His fame

went throughout all Syria; and they brought to Him all sick people

who were afflicted with various diseases and torments, and those

who were demon-possessed, epileptics, and paralytics; and He healed

them. Great multitudes followed Him—from Galilee, and from

Decapolis, Jerusalem, Judea, and beyond the Jordan. Then Jesus

went about all the cities and villages, teaching in their synagogues,

preaching the gospel of the kingdom, and healing every sickness and

every disease among the people. [77]

Every manifestation of the kingdom's power and authority was a blow against the head of the serpent.

Jesus' message and authority became a significant issue to the religious leaders of Israel. "What power and authority does He use to do these things," they wondered? Some concluded that Jesus cast out devils by the powers of darkness and not the power of heaven. A public confrontation took place one day in a synagogue.

Then one was brought to Him who was demon-possessed, blind and

mute; and He healed him so that the blind and mute man both

spoke and saw. And all the multitudes were amazed and said,

'Could this be the Son of David?' Now when the Pharisees heard it

they said, 'This fellow does not cast out demons except by

Beelzebub, the ruler of the demons.'" [78]

71

Jesus knew their hearts and the questions with which they were wrestling. He pointedly addressed them with the truth of the kingdom encounter they were beholding before their very eyes.

> *But Jesus knew their thoughts, and said to them: 'Every kingdom*
> *divided against itself is brought to desolation, and every city or house*
> *divided against itself will not stand. If Satan casts out Satan, he is*
> *divided against himself. How then will his kingdom stand? And if*
> *I cast out demons by Beelzebub, by whom do your sons cast them*
> *out? Therefore, they shall be your judges. But if I cast out demons*
> *by the Spirit of God, surely the kingdom of God has come upon*
> *you. Or how can one enter a strong man's house and plunder his*
> *goods, unless he first binds the strong man? And then he will*
> *plunder his house.* [79]

The Last Adam Encounters the Serpent of Hell

The very purpose of Jesus' coming was to plunder Satan's house. He came in the power of the Holy Spirit to bind the strong man of darkness and with the authority of God's throne, take all of his goods. Everywhere Jesus went he was destroying the works of the Devil (1 John 3:8) and preaching the gospel to the poor; healing the brokenhearted; proclaiming liberty to the captives and recovery of sight to the blind; setting at liberty those who are oppressed; and proclaiming the acceptable year of the LORD (Luke 4:18-19). The Apostle Peter told those gathered at the house of Cornelius "…how God anointed Jesus of Nazareth with the Holy Spirit and with power, who went about doing good and healing all who were oppressed by the devil, for God was with Him." [80]

Jesus' greatest confrontation with the powers of darkness came the night He was betrayed. He gathered with His followers for the Passover Seder, to which He had looked forward with great anticipation (Luke 22:15). Even there, at the most sacred of Jewish gatherings with His loyal followers, Jesus faced Satan in one of His own men. Earlier in the week plans had been laid for the betrayal of Jesus to the religious leaders of Jerusalem.

> *And Satan entered into Judas who was called Iscariot, belonging to the number of the twelve. And he went away and discussed with the chief priests and officers how he might betray Him to them. And they were glad, and agreed to give him money.* [81]

Satan came and filled Judas' heart, while sitting at the table with Jesus and the other disciples. He left the Seder early to complete his satanic assignment.

> *And having dipped the bread, he gave it to Judas Iscariot, the son of Simon. Now after the piece of bread, Satan entered him. Then Jesus said to him, 'What you do, do quickly.'* [82]

When the Seder was ended, Jesus led the disciples to the Garden of Gethsemane, on the Mount of Olives, for prayer. It was in a garden four millennia earlier that the first Adam faced satanic powers and lost. The Last Adam was now facing the hellish hounds in another garden; battling human will against divine will. The natural force of the human mind and body fought ardently against the events facing Jesus over the next seventy-two hours. Every form of human and natural desire screamed out against Him fulfilling the events that lay ahead. Demons animated every human emotion

73

and physical impulse. Satan left no stone unturned. Human reason and thought patterns were attacked by demonic distortion and every imagination of the mind became a cinema of satanic cunning. The Old Dragon pressed his advantage against Jesus' human will with every force he could muster from the regions of hell.

> *Then Jesus came with them to a place called Gethsemane, and said to His disciples, "Sit here while I go over there and pray. "And he took with Him Peter and the two songs of Zebedee, and began to be grieved and distressed. Then He said to them, "My soul is deeply grieved, to the point of death; remain here and keep watch with Me. " And He went a little beyond them, and fell on His face and prayed, saying, "My Father, if it is possible, let this cup pass from Me; yet not as I will, but as Thou wilt. " …He went away again a second time and prayed saying, "My Father, if this cannot pass away unless I drink it, Thy will be done. " …And He left them again, and went away and prayed a third time, saying the same thing once more.* [83]

> *Hour after hour, Jesus wrestled the powers of Hell to bring His own will in submission to the will of His Father. His body broke with the agony and blood began to dot his forehead, face, neck and arms where sweat should naturally have appeared. It was a horrible scene of raging spiritual war; light and darkness; truth against lie; love against hate; God fighting the forces of Lucifer for the souls of mankind.*

> *Surrender to the will of the Father was the only option, for earlier in*

the evening the cup of redemption had been lifted by the Son of Man and drained.

Then He took the cup, and gave thanks, and gave it to them, saying, "Drink from it, all of you. For this is My blood of the new covenant, which is shed for many for the remission of sins.[84]

The whole of creation groaned in agony hoping over that battle. It was longing for the redemption of mankind and the restoration of their God-given stewardship.

Another major blow was dealt to the kingdom of darkness as Jesus' human will surrendered to the will of Heavenly Father in the agony of those hours in the Garden of Gethsemane. The stage was now set of the total defeat of Satan and his demonic host.

Every event that filled the next three days in Jesus' life was a mortal blow by the kingdom of God, crushing the head of the serpent and bringing eternal redemption to the human race (Matthew 26:56). Isaiah, the prophet, recorded these events seven centuries beforehand.

But he was wounded for our transgressions, he was bruised for our iniquities: the chastisement of our peace was upon him; and with his stripes we are healed. All we like sheep, have gone astray; we have turned everyone to his own way; and the LORD hath laid on him the iniquity of us all. He was oppressed, and he was afflicted, yet he opened not his mouth: he is brought as a lamb to the slaughter, and as a sheep before her shearers is dumb, so he openeth not his mouth. [85]

Seven Bruises to the Heel

Jesus Christ experienced the worst torture and agony Satan could conjure in the hearts of men. Lucifer used the Jewish and Roman authorities to inflict his bruises upon the heel of the "Seed of Woman" (Gen. 3:15). He failed to recognize it would also be the demise of his own kingdom.

Demons lied through false witnesses; agitated the general public; belittled Jesus through the games and mockery of the Roman soldiers; stirred the crowd to choose a guilty murderer over the innocent Son of God; and then convinced Pontius Pilate he could order his crucifixion but remain innocent if he just washed his hands after giving the sentence.

Arrested and Imprisoned for All Mankind

"Judas, are you betraying the Son of Man with a kiss," asked Jesus,[86] as the betrayer signaled the temple guards by his act of friendship. Jesus was taken from the Garden of Gethsemane to the home of Caiaphas, the High Priest and imprisoned in the dungeon until the religious counsel met the next morning.

> *"As soon as it was day, the elders of the people, both chief priests and scribes, came together and led Him into their council."*[87]

Three and a half years earlier, Jesus had declared His mission to free the captives. "The Spirit of the Lord is upon Me, because he anointed Me to preach the gospel to the poor. He has sent Me to proclaim release to the captives." (Luke 4:18 NAS) His ministry freed captives one person at a time, as He cast out demons, healed the sick and afflicted, and forgave the sins of the immoral and outcast of society.

The night of his arrest and imprisonment, the stage was being set for Him to open the prison doors for all humanity in one great act of deliverance. The Apostle declared the power and authority of Jesus' great deliverance.

> *For He delivered us from the domain of darkness, and transferred*
> *us to the kingdom of His Beloved Son, in whom we have*
> *redemption, the forgiveness of sins.*[88]

Beaten to Free Mankind from Iniquity

The temple guards spit in Jesus' face; covered his eyes with a blindfold then hit Him with their fists; all this while calling out, "Prophesy, Christ, who just hit you" (Matthew 26:67; Mark 14:65). The Roman soldiers mocked Him and beat Him unmercifully, bruising His face almost beyond recognition. They pulled His beard out by the roots; shoved a crown of thorns on His head; placed a Roman robe around his shoulders; put a staff in His hand and hailed Him in mockery as King of the Jews; then hit Him on the head again and again with the staff.

All of this punishment was exacted upon Jesus Christ to purchase the forgiveness of mankind's iniquitous actions against God. Since Adam and Eve's sin in the garden, the iniquity of fathers has been passed to the third and fourth generation of their children (Exodus 20:5, 34:7). God said, "But your iniquities have made a separation between you and your God and your sins have hidden His face from you.[89] The Apostle Paul said we make ourselves slaves to iniquity (Romans 6:19).

Gesenius defines iniquity as "perversity, depravity...guilt contracted by sinning."[90] Harris, Archer and Waltke agree saying, "The basic meaning of the verb, 'to bend, twist, distort...' from this primary notion it derives the sense 'to distort, to make crooked, to pervert....' When the distortion pertains to law it means 'to sin, to infract, to commit a perversion / iniquity....' It denotes both the deed and its consequences, the misdeed and its punishment."[91] In the New Testament iniquity is the Greek word for *anomia* meaning, "without law because ignorant of it [or] because of violation of it. Contempt and violation of the law.... Wickedness." [92]

Man's self-willed living causes him to have contempt for the law of God and to pervert it. The bruises and lacerations Jesus suffered the night of His betrayal and on the day of His trial brought deliverance to mankind from the judgment of their iniquity. Isaiah, the prophet, declared, "He was bruised for our iniquity."

> *Jesus Christ who gave himself for us, that he might redeem us from all iniquity, and purify unto Himself a peculiar people, zealous of good works. These things speak, and exhort, and rebuke with all authority. Let no man despise thee.*[93]

Falsely Accused to Justify Mankind

Witness after witness was brought before the High Priest and Jewish religious counsel in an attempt to establish the crime and guilt of Jesus Christ.

Now the chief priests, and elders, and all the council, sought false
witness against Jesus, to put him to death; But found none: yea,
though many false witnesses came, yet found they none....[94]

At last they found two liars who came before the High Priest giving false
evidence that Jesus had spoken against the temple of the living God. Jesus
did not answer His false accusers. Exasperated, the High Priest stood and
declared, "I adjure thee by the living God, that thou tell us whether thou be
the Christ, the Son of God" (Matthew 26:63 KJV). Jesus had to answer the
true accusation saying, "Thou hast said: nevertheless, I say unto you,
Hereafter shall ye see the Son of man sitting on the right hand of power, and
coming in the clouds of Heaven" (Matthew 26:64 KJV). The High Priest
became enraged and accused Jesus of blasphemy. He then violated the
Mosaic Law by tearing His priestly garment.

And Moses said unto Aaron, and unto Eleazar and unto
Ithamar, his sons, Uncover not your heads, neither rend your
clothes; lest ye die, and lest wrath come upon all the people: but let
your brethren, the whole house of Israel, bewail the burning which
the LORD hath kindled.[95]

And he that is the high priest among his brethren, upon whose head
the anointing oil was poured, and that is consecrated to put on the
garments, shall not uncover his head, nor rend his clothes[96]

The High Priest tearing his garments was a critical sign of what had just taken
place in the council meeting. The Eternal High Priest had been identified and
the ministry of the earthly High Priest brought to an end. Most men in the

religious counsel did not recognize the true meaning of those events. I am not certain the High Priest, himself, recognized the magnitude and meaning of what he had just done. The visible reality of those events would not be felt for some years to come, when the Roman army would destroy the earthly temple and priesthood. The spiritual reality of these events was seen immediately.

Jesus was then taken before the Roman Procurator, Pontius Pilate, after the Sanhedrin found Him guilty of blasphemy. Pilate sent Him to Herod, the hated Jewish King. Herod then sent Jesus back to Pontius Pilate for final sentencing (Luke 23:1-11).

Before Pilate again, Jesus was found innocent of all charges.

> *Ye have brought this man unto me, as one that perverteth the*
> *people: and, behold, I, having examined Him before you, have*
> *found no fault in this man touching those things whereof ye accuse*
> *him: No, nor yet Herod: for I sent you to him; and, lo, nothing*
> *worthy of death is done unto Him. I will therefore chastise Him,*
> *and release Him.* [97]

The Sanhedrin would not be satisfied. They pressed the Roman Procurator to execute Jesus. Pilate finally gave in and gave the people a choice.

> *Now at the feast, the governor was wont to release unto the people a*
> *prisoner, whom they would. And they had then a notable prisoner,*
> *called Barabbas. Therefore, when they were gathered together,*
> *Pilate said unto them, "Whom will ye that I release unto you?*

Barabbas, or Jesus which is called Christ?" For he knew that for
envy they had delivered Him. Then he was set down on the
judgment seat, his wife sent unto him, saying, "Have thou nothing
to do with that just man: for I have suffered many things this day
in a dream because of Him." But the chief priests and elders
persuaded the multitude that they should ask Barabbas, and destroy
Jesus. The governor answered and said unto them, "Whether of the
twain will ye that I release unto you?" They said, Barabbas. Pilate
saith unto them, "What shall I do then with Jesus which is called
Christ?" They all say unto him, "Let Him be crucified." And the
governor said, "Why, what evil hath He done?" But they cried out
the more, saying, "Let him be crucified." When Pilate saw that he
could prevail nothing, but that rather a tumult was made, he took
water, and washed his hands before the multitude, saying, "I am
innocent of the blood of this just person: see ye to it." Then
answered all the people, and said, "His blood be on us, and on our
children." Then released he Barabbas unto them: and when he had
scourged Jesus, he delivered Him to be crucified.[98]

The people willingly exchanged the innocent for the guilty. The stage was set
for the greatest event in the history of mankind.

The trials of Jesus by the Sanhedrin and by the Roman government were the
initial steps of the Eternal High Priest providing justification for mankind;
who stands accused and found guilty before Almighty God, as hopeless and
habitual sinners. "For all have sinned and come short of the glory of God"
(Romans 6:23).

There is none righteous, no not one. There is none that understandeth, there is none that seeketh after God. They are all gone out of the way, they are together become unprofitable; there is none that doeth good, no, not one. Their throat is an open sepulcher; with their tongues they have used deceit; the poison of asps is under their lips: Whose mouth is full of cursing and bitterness: Their feet are swift to shed blood: Destruction and misery are in their ways: And the way of peace have they not known: There is no fear of God before their eyes. [99]

And I saw a great white throne, and him that sat on it, from whose face the earth and the heaven fled away; and there was found no place for them. And I saw the dead, small and great, stand before God; and the books were opened: and another book was opened, which is the Book of Life: and the dead were judged out of those things which were written in the books, according to their works. And the sea gave up the dead which were in it; and death and hell delivered up the dead which were in them: and they were judged every man according to their works. And death and hell were cast into the Lake of Fire. This is the second death. And whosoever was not found written in the Book of Life was cast into the Lake of Fire. [100]

Mankind could do nothing to free himself from the guilt and the judgment pronounced against him. From the Garden of Eden man was guilty and looking for the day when his guilt would finally be removed forever by the "Seed of Women." That day had finally arrived.

But God commendeth his love toward us, in that, while we were yet

sinners, Christ died for us. Much more than, being now justified by

his blood we shall be saved from wrath through him. [101]

Justification is the judicial action by which Almighty God declares a person to be just as if they had never sinned. The Greek word is *dikaioo* meaning "to render righteous." [102] Jesus Christ's substitutionary work through the Jewish and Roman trials, made it possible for a human being to be declared righteous through divine fiat. The Apostle Paul said, "He made Him who knew no sin to be sin on our behalf, that we might become the righteousness of God in Him" (2 Cor. 5:21 NAS).

We have to be quite clear that the word justify, used in this sense,

has a quite different meaning from its ordinary English meaning. If

we justify ourselves, we produce reasons to prove that we were right.

If someone justifies us he produces reasons to prove that we did it in

the right way. But all verbs in Greek which end in oó do not mean

to prove a person or things to be something, or to make a person or

thing to be something; they always mean to treat, or account or

reckon a person to be something. Now if God justifies the sinner, it

does not mean that He finds reasons to prove that the sinner was

right - far from it. It does not mean that, at this point, He even

makes the sinner a good man. What it does mean is that God

treats the sinner as if he had not been a sinner at all. Instead of

treating the sinner as a criminal to be obliterated, God treats him as

a child to be loved. That is what justification means. It means that

God reckons us not as His enemies but as His friends, that God

treats us not as bad men deserve, but as good men deserve. It means

He looks on us not as law-breakers to be punished, but as men and
women only to be loved. That is the very essence of the gospel.[103]

Flogged for the Healing of Mankind

Then Pilate, when he had called together the chief priests, the rulers,
and the people, said to them, "You have brought this Man to me,
as one who misleads the people. And indeed, having examined
Him in your presence, I have found no fault in this Man concerning
those things of which you accuse Him; no, neither did Herod, for I
sent you back to him; and indeed nothing deserving of death has
been done by Him. I will therefore chastise Him and release Him. [104]

Jesus was subsequently flogged by the Roman guards for crimes he had not
committed. The Prophet Isaiah referred to this awful moment of torture and
agony as part of the redemptive work for mankind.

He is despised and rejected of men; a man of sorrows, and
acquainted with grief: and we hid as it were our faces from him; he
was despised, and we esteemed him not. Surely he hath borne our
griefs, and carried our sorrows: yet we did esteem him stricken,
smitten of God, and afflicted… and with his stripes we are healed. [105]

There are two very revealing Hebrew words found in this passage by Isaiah.
  ➤ Sorrows – *mak'ob* – "pain"

84

➤ Grief – *choily* – "disease" [106]

Picture in your mind the suffering of Jesus Christ. He has experienced the physical torture of the agonizing prayer in the Garden of Gethsemane. He is in pain from the beatings of the temple guards. As the Roman guards tied Him to the flogging post, the pain and agony of the sickness and diseases experienced by the human race came in full force upon His body.

Preparations for the scourging are carried out. The prisoner is stripped of His clothing and His hands tied to a post above His head. The Roman legionnaire steps forwards with the flagrum in his hand. This is a short whip consisting of several heavy, leather thongs with two small balls of lead attached near the ends of each. The heavy whip is brought down with the full force again and again across Jesus' shoulders, back and legs. At first the heavy thongs cut through skin only. Then, as the blows continue, they cut deeper into the subcutaneous tissues, producing first an oozing of blood from the capillaries and veins of the skin, and finally spurting arterial bleeding from vessels in the underlying muscles. The small balls of lead first produce large, deep bruises, which are broken open by the subsequent blows.

Finally, the skin of the back is hanging in long ribbons and the entire area is an unrecognizable mass of torn bleeding tissue. When it is determined by the centurion in charge that the prisoner is near death, the beating is finally stopped. The half-fainting Jesus is then

untied and allowed to slump to the stone pavement, wet with His
own blood. [107]

Sickness and disease has wracked the human body since the fall of Adam and Even in the Garden of Eden. When God delivered Israel out of Egypt, He proclaimed Himself to be Jehovah-Ropheka, "the Lord that healeth thee" (Exodus 15:26). The prophet Isaiah assured that every cut made by the Roman scourge on the body of our Lord Jesus Christ was purchasing healing for the sickness, disease and broken bodies of mankind.

The Apostle Peter referred to this passage by the Prophet when he declared, "… by whose stripes ye were healed." The Apostle refers to the healing as past tense, an accomplished fact. Indeed, it is! Healing was won for all those who will receive it by faith, through the suffering of our Lord at the flogging post in the Tower of Antonia.

Crucified as the Eternal Lamb of God

Finding great sport in this simple man claiming to be a king, the whole garrison of Roman soldiers gathers around as He is taken from the scourging post. The hard bitten soldiers threw a scarlet robe around His shoulders; put a stick in the blood covered hand for a make-believe scepter; then made a crown for Him out of branches from a thorn bush. As they pressed the ridiculous crown upon His head, the thorns punctured many of the blood vessels in the scalp and blood began streaming down Jesus' face and neck.

The mockery continued as the laughing, playful soldier began kneeling before the Son of God yelling, "Hail, King of the Jews." These war hardened soldiers had seen many governors and rulers defeated in war. They could hardly imagine this weak and passive Jew being a king of any kind. The mock-scepter was taken from His hand and used to beat Him about the head and shoulders while other soldiers spit on him. They stripped Him of the "royal robe" and put Hs own blood soaked clothes back on and led Him off to be crucified (Mathew 27:27-31).

The slow procession of the Roman execution detail, composed of two thieves, the so-called Jewish king and the soldier, made their way from the Praetorium to Calvary. The heavy wooden beam of crucifixion had been placed across the shoulders of each condemned man. The wood dug deep into the lacerations and the exposed muscles and ligaments in Jesus back. Loss of sleep, copious bleeding and the physical torture had taken its toll. He fell under the weight of the wooden beam. A man in the crowd, Simon of Cyrene, was forced to pick up the beam and carry it. When they arrived at the hill of execution called Golgotha, Place of the Skull, the condemned were placed on each of the crosses.

> *At Golgotha, the beam is placed on the ground and Jesus is quickly thrown backward with His shoulders against the wood. The legionnaire feels for the depression at the front of the wrist. He drives a heavy, square, wrought-iron nail through the wrist and deep into the wood. Quickly, he moves to the other side and repeats the action, being careful not to pull the arms too tightly, but to allow some flexion and movement. The beam is then lifted in place at the top of the posts and the titulus reading "Jesus of Nazareth, King of the Jews" is nailed in place.*

The left foot is pressed backward against the right foot, and with both feet extended, toes down, a nail is driven through the arch of each as He pushes Himself upward to avoid the stretching torment, He places His full weight on the nail through His feet. Again there is the searing agony of the nail tearing through the nerves between the metatarsal bones of the feet.

As the arms fatigue, great waves of cramps sweep over the muscles knotting them in deep, relentless, throbbing pain. With these cramps comes the inability to push Himself upward. Hanging by His arms…air can be drawn into the lungs, but cannot be exhaled…carbon dioxide builds up in the lungs and in the blood stream….

The compressed heart is struggling to pump heavy, thick, sluggish blood into the tissues—the tortured lungs are making a frantic effort to gasp in small gulps of air. The markedly dehydrated tissues send their flood of stimuli to the brain. Jesus gasps, "I thirst."

He can feel the chill of death creeping through His tissues. With one last surge of strength He… utters His seventh and last cry, "Father, into Thy hands I commit my spirit."

Apparently to make doubly sure of death, the legionnaire drove his lance through the fifth interspace between the ribs, upward through the pericardium and into the heart. Immediately there came out blood and water. We, therefore, have rather conclusive post-mortem evidence that our Lord died, not the usual crucifixion death by

88

suffocation, but of heart failure due to shock and constriction of the heart by fluid in the pericardium." [108]

Watching this whole scene were the Roman soldiers who had been mocking and spitting upon Jesus just hours before. Suddenly, the earth shook; rocks were split open and thrown around. Thick darkness covered the sun and terror filled the hearts of the people watching (Matthew 27:51; Luke 24:44-49).

One of the soldiers, a centurion, was overcome with the emotion of what he had been witnessing and cried out, "Truly this was the Son of God."[109] Imagine the horror of that realization. Earlier in the day, he and his men had been mocking, laughing, spitting on and ridiculing this very man, whom he now knew to be the Son of God. The realization that came to the heart of the Roman Centurion on Golgotha that day is the only hope for mankind.

The horrible scene of torture and death that took place on Calvary is the very purpose for which Jesus Christ came to earth. Again quoting that great prophet Isaiah,

> *But He was pierced through for our transgressions, He was crushed for our iniquities; the chastening for our well-being {fell} upon Him, and by His scourging we are healed. All of us like sheep have gone astray, each of us has turned to his own way; but the LORD has caused the iniquity of us all to fall on Him.* [110]

Jesus' death on the cross was the eternal sacrifice for the sins of mankind. The physical suffering of crucifixion was compounded for Jesus Christ by His carrying the weight of humanity's sin in His own body on the tree. Peter wrote in his first epistle, "He, Himself, bore our sins in His body on the tree that we might die to sin and live for righteousness" (1 Peter 2:24 NIV). The Apostle Paul explained to the saints at Corinth the significance of Jesus Christ carrying the sins of mankind.

> *To wit, that God was in Christ, reconciling the world unto Himself, not imputing their trespasses unto them; and hath committed unto us the word of reconciliation. Now then we are ambassadors for Christ, as though God did beseech you by us: we pray you in Christ's stead, be ye reconciled to God. For He hath made Him to be sin for us, who knew no sin; that we might be made the righteousness of God in Him.*[111]

Jesus Was Buried in a Borrowed Tomb

Near evening the body of Jesus was taken from the cross and buried in a borrowed tomb. Malcolm Muggeridge describes the scene.

> *The first manifestation of Jesus's [sic] presence in the world came immediately after his death. Thanks to one of his rich secret followers, Joseph of Arimathea, a new tomb hollowed out of a rock was available for Jesus's body, and permission was given for Him to be laid in it. With the help of another of his wealthy followers,*
>
> *Nicodemus, the body was hurriedly embalmed and wrapped in linen bands. A large stone was placed in position to close the mouth of the tomb, and guards were posted to ensure that no attempt was made to remove the body in order to claim that, as He had*

prophesied, Jesus had risen from the dead. None the less, when at
midnight the following day three women came to the tomb, they
found the stone rolled away and Jesus's body removed. Thereafter
Jesus appeared on numerous occasions, in his bodily shape and with
his bodily needs.[112]

Jesus spent three days in the borrowed tomb, during which time He went to the regions of the sheol (Acts 2:22-27). Duffield and Van Cleave explain:

After the resurrection of Jesus, the abode of the righteous was
transferred from Sheol to Paradise. Jesus personally descended into
Sheol to 'lead captivity captive' (Ephesians 4:8). He spent'…three
days and three nights in the heart of the earth' (Matthew 12:40 –
apparently Sheol is located in the heart of the earth.) (Also
Ephesians 4:9-10; Numbers 16:33).[113]

The Kingdom of God Extended

MR. PRINCIPLE, *your Imminence, your Disgraces, my Thorns, Shadies, and Gentledevils:*

...But now for the pleasant part of my duty. It falls to my lot to propose on behalf of the guests the health of Principle Slubgob and the Tempters' Training college. Fill your glasses. What is this I see? What is this delicious bouquet I inhale? Can it be? . . . old vintage Pharisee. Well, well, well. This is like old times. Hold it beneath your nostrils for a moment, gentledevils. Hold it up to the light. Look at those fiery streaks that writhe and tangle in its dark heart, as if they were contending. And so they are. You know how this wine is blended? Different types of Pharisee have been harvested, trodden, and fermented together to produce its subtle flavour. Types that were most antagonistic to one another on Earth. Some were all rules and relics and rosaries; others were all drab clothes, long faces and petty traditional abstinences from wine or cards or the theatre. Both had in common their self-righteousness and the almost infinite distance between their actual outlook and anything the Enemy really is or commands...

Your Imminence, your Disgraces, my Thorns, Shadies and Gentledevils:
I give you the toast of -
Principal Slubgob and the College!
Lewis, The Screwtape Letters

"I will destroy you and your family!"

I awoke with a start; then heard the voice and those words once again.

"I will destroy you and your family!"

I had been in a sound sleep, in our new home. My wife and I had started a new church plant just weeks before. God's blessings were flowing, as new families were attending and souls were being saved. What was happening? My head was still muddled from sleep, still, the chill of those words hung in the air.

The icy terror of such an awakening was only matched by the cold dank air of the demonic presence that filled our house. I slipped out of bed into my robe and slippers.

Quietly, I moved from the master bedroom into the hall. The foreboding presence was suffocating. My children were sleeping quietly upstairs, as I moved into the living room. "God, I cry to you and plead the blood of Jesus," I prayed.

Again, the voice called out, "We will destroy you. You have no power over us." It seemed a hundred demons had filled our home. Power surged within me! Boldness filled my heart and my voice, as I shouted in a whisper, "You have no power here! You have no power over me and my family. We belong to the Lord Jesus Christ and His blood covers our home and our lives. I command you in Jesus' name; leave this house and this property, now!" The battle of demonic will and intimidation raged for several minutes. Standing firm in faith and confidence, I knew the demonic forces must humble themselves at the name of Jesus Christ and leave our home. I would allow nothing less! As a blood-bought child of the Almighty God, I drove them out and they never came back.

I returned to a good night's sleep. The next morning, neither my wife nor my children were aware of anything that had happened in the night season.

It Truly Is a War

We are at war. It is not a shooting war like *Saving Private Ryan*, the Ho Chi Minh Trail, or 9/11/2001 in New York City. The war we fight is a spiritual war fought between two kingdoms; the kingdom of God and the kingdom of Satan. It is a war for the souls of mankind; the culture of people; and the future of nations.

It is a war fought on the battleground of each individual mind and heart. It is a war fought every day on school campuses and neighborhood streets. It is a war fought in the homes and work places. It is a war fought in the halls of government. It is a battle for marriages, the lives of children, arts and literature, truth and right, and the very soul of a nation. It is a war to which God has called every believer. *It is a call from which we must not shrink or fail to answer!*

Are you a believer? If you are, then you are in combat with demon personalities! John Hagee and E. M. Bounds both agree that the church in modern day has signed a peace treaty with the devil and his demons when all along there needs to be a declaration of war. Hagee tells a funny story.

'It's the story of a building contractor in Texas who did some work at the church and was having a hard time collecting his fee. So he rented a red phosphorous devil suit, the kind that glows in the dark. One Sunday night while the service was going on, he entered the back of the church, put on the suit and sneaked over to where the

light paneling was located. The precise moment, he switched off all the lights and sprang onto the platform roaring like a lion. The bright moonlight caused the red phosphorous suit to glow in the dark. The people ran in terror. A stampede for the door began with the Pastor leading the way. There was one feeble old lady who was unable to run with the rest, so she knelt down at the feet of the contractor-turned-devil. "Oh, Mr. Devil," she said, "I have worked in this Sunday School class, baked pies for every bake sale, and even cut the grass when I was younger. But in spite of all that, Mr. Devil, I want you to know from the bottom of my heart I was on your side all the time!"

It's really time that the church makes a choice; dignity or deliverance. The church needs to deal with demons that control the people. It's time to recognize demons and declare war against them.[114]

A Call to Arms

Winston Churchill gave one of his most important speeches to the House of Commons on May 13, 1940. England had been at war with Germany for ten months. It was not a war Britain wanted or sought after. In fact, Prime Minister Chamberlain had tried every means of negotiation available. Germany had thrust this war upon her.

Austria had been over run in a single night. Germany had broken faith with world leaders and taken Sudetenland, eventually swallowing up the entire Czechoslovakian Republic. The Blitzkrieg slaughtered Poland, took Denmark, Norway, Luxembourg, Belgium, France, and Holland.

Next the *Luftwaffe* was heard over the Isles of Great Britain. Daily it rained terror upon her cities and villages. The Parliament of Britain thrust aside the appeasement policy of Neville Chamberlain and accepted the bull dog leadership of Winston Churchill. His first address to the Parliament of Britain resounded with great resolve.

> *I would say to the house, as I have said to those who have joined this government: 'I have nothing to offer but blood, toil, tears and sweat.' We have before us an ordeal of the most grievous kind. We have before us many, many long months of struggle and of suffering. You ask, what is our policy? I will say: it is to wage war, by sea, land and air, with all our might and with all the strength that God can give us: to wage war against a monstrous tyranny never surpassed in the dark, lamentable catalogue of human crime. That is our policy.*
>
> *You ask What is our aim? I can answer in one word: Victory. Victory at all costs, victory in spite of all terror, victory, however long, and hard the road may be; for without victory, there is no survival. Let that be realized; no survival for the British Empire; no survival for all that the British Empire has stood for, no survival for the urge and impulses of the ages, that mankind will move forward towards its goal. But I take up my task with buoyancy and hope. I feel sure that our cause will not be suffered to fail among men. At this time, I feel entitled to claim the aid of all, and I say, 'Come, then, let us go forward together with our united strength.'*[115]

That must be the heart and the spirit of the church of Jesus Christ. We are at war and "without victory there is no survival." Every culture, every city, every hamlet, every village, every human being will be destroyed by the evil powers of darkness, unless the church rises up in the power and authority of God's Kingdom and displaces every vestige of hell's influence and dominion.

The Kingdom of God Must Be Pressed Forward

John the Baptist had been imprisoned by Herod Antipas. During his days of imprisonment, he had begun to question whether he really had baptized the Messiah. The weary prophet sent messengers to Jesus asking, "Are you the coming one or do we look for another." The Son of God responded, "Go and tell John, the blind see; the lame walk; the lepers are cleansed; and the deaf hear; the dead are raised up and the poor have the gospel preached to them."

As these men departed, Jesus made an astounding statement, "And from the days of John the Baptist until now the kingdom of heaven suffereth violence, and the violent take it by force."[116] He made a similar statement some time later addressing the hypocrisy of religious leaders. "The law and the prophets were until John. Since that time the kingdom of God has been preached, and everyone is pressing into it."[117]

There was no question in Jesus' mind. He was in the middle of a spiritual war between the kingdom of God and the kingdom of Satan. The conflict must be "pressed" if God' kingdom is to be advanced. Dr. Jack Hayford has written a footnote to Matthew 11:12 in the *Spirit-Filled Life Bible.*

*Though the Greek here is somewhat difficult to translate, the idea in this verse is that **the kingdom of heaven**, which Jesus set up as a powerful movement or reign among men (**suffers violence**), requires of them an equally strong and radical reaction. **The violent** then **who take it by force** are people of keen enthusiasm and commitment who are willing to respond to and propagate with radical abandonment the message and dynamic of God's reign... [author's emphasis]*[118]

Jesus pressed this point home to the twelve disciples when He explained:

Behold, I send you out as sheep in the midst of wolves; therefore, be shrewd as serpents, and innocent as doves. But beware of men; for they will deliver you up to the courts, and scourge you in their synagogues; and you shall even be brought before governors and kings for My sake, as a testimony to them and to the Gentiles. But when they deliver you up, do not become anxious about how or what you will speak; for it shall be given you in that hour what you are to speak. For it is not you who speak, but it is the Spirit of your Father who speaks in you. And brother will deliver up brother to death, and a father his child; and children will rise up against parents, and cause them to be put to death. And you will be hated by all on account of My name, but it is the one who has endured to the end who will be saved.[119]

To seventy other disciples He said, "The harvest truly is great, but the laborers are few; therefore, pray the Lord of the harvest to send out laborers into His harvest. Go your way; behold, I send you out as lambs among wolves."

What Power and Authority Would "Press" the Kingdom?

Jesus took the twelve disciples to Northern Galilee for a time of refreshing and personal teaching. They stayed at the head waters of the Jordan River, a resort community built by Philip, the son of Herod the Great. He named the community Caesarea Philippi, in honor of the Roman ruler Caesar. Antiquity had known the location for worship of the god Pan. A grotto was carved into the massive cave, from which the head waters flow. An inscription still testifies to the center of worship.

When Jesus brought His disciples to this lovely resort city,

> *"Two religious systems were carried on together. Pan was worshiped*
> *in the grotto, while Caesar was worshipped in the white temple that*
> *probably stood on the cliff above, the site of the present Muslim*
> *shrine of Sheikh Jhudr, or St. George. The exact location of*
> *Herod's temple is not known. Building stones are strewn all around*
> *the area."*[20]

It was at this scene of obvious idolatrous worship Jesus wanted His disciples to receive an important lesson. He began with a question. "Who do men say that I am?" Their answers varied, at first. "Some say John the Baptist, others say Elijah, Jeremiah or one of the prophets." Jesus became more pointed with His question. "But, who do you say that I am?" It was Simon Peter who answered Him directly. "You are the Christ, the Son of the Living God" (Matthew 16:1-17).

100

That was the answer for which Jesus was looking. With that revelation He could establish three great truths that would be the foundation upon which the church of Jesus Christ would be built and the authority to fulfill its mission.

> *Blessed are you, Simon Bar-Jonah, for flesh and blood has not revealed this to you, but My Father who is in heaven. And I also say to you that you are Peter, and on this rock I will build My church, and the gates of Hades shall not prevail against it. And I will give you the keys of the kingdom of heaven, and whatever you bind on earth will be bound in heaven, and whatever you loose on earth will be loosed in heaven."*[21]

The truths found in this teaching are some of the most profound, yet, controversial lessons Jesus taught during His ministry.

The true identity of Jesus Christ is the foundation stone of the Church. Roman Catholicism teaches this passage declares the Apostle Peter to be the foundation stone of the Church. That is not scripturally correct. The Apostle Paul said, "For no other foundation can anyone lay than that which is laid, which is Jesus Christ."[122] Power and the authority are not given to the church in the name of Peter but through the name of Jesus Christ. The seventy other disciples came home from their missions saying, "Lord, even the demons are subject to us *in Your name* [emphasis mine]."[123] Jesus said, "And whatsoever ye ask in My name, that will I do, that the Father may be glorified in the Son. If ye ask anything in My name, I will do it."[124] He told the church to "Go ye into all the world and preach the gospel to every creature. And these signs shall follow them that believe; in my Name they shall cast out devils; they shall speak with new tongues."[125] "Neither is there salvation in any other: for there is none other name under heaven given among men, whereby we must be saved."[126] "And He is the head of the body, the church: who is the beginning, the firstborn from the dead; that in all things He might have the preeminence."[127] The one true foundation of the church is Jesus Christ, Himself, and no other.

The purpose for which the church has been built was also clearly stated by Jesus Christ. "And the gates of hell shall not prevail against it." The church is to violently press against the gates of hell everywhere she finds a stronghold of darkness. The church was never meant to be a defensive fortress in which the saints hide secure, in a holy huddle waiting for Jesus return. God promised in Isaiah 54:17. "No weapon formed against you shall prosper." The Apostle Paul declared, "If God is for us, who can be against us... Yet in all these things we are more than conquerors through Him that loved us."[128] The church was designed and created to be on the offensive and to prevail in taking the territories and strongholds hell may hold in this world. Jesus assured the gates would break open and the strongholds of hell plundered.

Jesus has given the keys of the kingdom of heaven to the church to bind the strongmen of hell and to loose the people being held in darkness. Examples of this truth are given to us in the Gospel of Matthew and in the Gospel of Luke. Jesus appointed twelve disciples to work with Him in the ministry and gave them authority to do eight things (Matthew 12:1-15): cast out devils, heal sickness and all kinds of disease, preach the kingdom of God was at hand, cleanse the leper, raise the dead, bless the homes in which they stayed with peace of God, bless or curse the city and villages to which they went, not to go to the Gentiles or the Samaritans, only to Israel.

Jesus appointed seventy disciples, in addition to the twelve, to go ahead of Him, into the cities and villages where He would soon come. When He commissioned them they were given authority to do four things (Luke 10:1-16): bless the homes in which they would stay with the peace of God, heal the sick, preach the kingdom of God has come to you, bless or curse the cities and villages to which they were going, they were not limited to Israeli cities and villages only, but they were to go "…into every city and place He, Himself, was about to go."

The seventy returned from their mission rejoicing because with the power and authority they had plundered the gates of hell. "And the seventy returned with joy, saying, Lord, even the demons are subject to us in Your name."[129] Jesus confirmed they did, indeed, have authority over the kingdom of Satan, *in His name.*

> *And He said to them, "I saw Satan fall like lightning from heaven. Behold, I give you the authority to trample on serpents and scorpions, and over all the power of the enemy, and nothing shall by any means hurt you.*[130]

The same authority Jesus gave to the twelve and to the seventy disciples has been given to the church for carrying out the Great Commission. Jesus said, 'Go into all the world and preach the gospel to every creature. He who believes and is baptized will be saved; but he who does not believe will be condemned."[131]

Notice the following points of similarity between the "Great Commission" and the commission Jesus gave to the twelve and to the seventy. Cast out devils, speak with new tongues, take up serpents, if they drink any deadly thing it shall not hurt them, lay hands on the sick and they shall recover, they were not limited to Israeli cities and villages or to the cities where Jesus would physically go. The church is to go "into all the world."[132]

The mission of the church in every generation is the same as that for which Jesus came from the Father.

> *The Spirit of the LORD is upon Me, Because He has anointed Me To preach the gospel to the poor; He has sent Me to heal the brokenhearted, To proclaim liberty to the captives And recovery of sight to the blind, To set at liberty those who are oppressed; To proclaim the acceptable year of the LORD.*[133]

The "Great Commission" of the church is to extend the kingdom of God around the world in the same manner He was extending the kingdom in each city, village and hamlet where He walked. He told the followers, "Verily, verily I say unto you, he that believeth in me the works that I do shall he do also and greater works than these shall he do because I go unto my Father" (John 14:12). The church is to go forth and plunder hell, freeing souls from the slavery of sin, the prisons of darkness and the bondages of disease. Jesus has given to the church the Great Commission to crush the very gates of hell.

This is a great cause and it demands a great choice. The church must not fail her sons and daughters, neighbors or friends. She must not let this generation pass without knowing the gospel of Jesus Christ and the glory of God. The church must not allow the powers of hell to dictate the terms and press the advantage.

Again, quoting the great British Statesman.

> *What is our aim? I can answer in one word:* **Victory.** *Victory*
> *at all costs, victory in spite of all terror, victory, however long, and*
> *hard the road may be;* ***for without victory, there is no***
> ***survival.***[134] *[my emphasis]*

Six days after his speech to Parliament, May 13, 1940, Churchill spoke to the nation on public radio saying, "Our task is not only to win the battle - but to win the war."[135] That must be the heart of the church. That must be her only aim! The church must rise to battle; take on the fight and press the enemy wherever she finds him: in the home, on the job or at the store; in broken lives with troubled minds and damaged emotions; while walking the neighborhoods, commuting to work, or at church.

It is time for war!

It is time to drive back the forces of darkness and to plunder hell!

The Weapons That Are Mighty

Through God

MR. PRINCIPLE, *Your Imminence, your Disgraces,*
my Thorns, Shadies, and Gentledevils:

... In each individual choice of what the Enemy would call the "wrong" turning, such
creatures are at first hardly, if at all, in a state of full spiritual responsibility. They do not
understand either the source of the real character of the prohibitions they are breaking. Their
consciousness hardly exits apart from the social atmosphere that surrounds them. And of
course we have contrived that their very language should be all smudge and blur; what would
be a bribe in someone else's profession is a tip or a present in theirs. The job of their
Tempters was first, of course, to harden these choices of the Hellward roads into a habit by
steady repetition. But then (and this was all-important) to turn the habit into a principle - a
principle the creature is prepared to defend. After that, all will go well...

Screwtape's reply to Dr. Slubgob's greeting, as guest of honor at the annual dinner of the
Tempter's Training College for young devils

Lewis, The Screwtape Letters

I had been the new Senior Pastor at an Oregon congregation for only a few
weeks. Certainly not adequate time to gain insight of the congregation and
community necessary for in-depth leadership and spiritual warfare. Yet, I
could not deny the awareness I had of an oppressive spirit every time I came

into the building. It was a level of oppression that could not be explained merely by the difficult circumstances these dear people had faced over a lengthy period of time. There were times this evil presence was suffocating to the praise and worship of the congregation and brought resistance to the ministry of the Word.

"Pastor I don't like going into the building at night. I won't go in there alone after dark. I am afraid. Do you feel a presence in the building, when you go in?" The young lady asking me that question was a member of the congregation. I understood what she was saying and the emotion with which she expressed it. "Yes, I am very aware of what you are describing. How long have you felt that way," I asked? "For a long time," she responded. I had experienced those same feelings but had not told anyone the level of spiritual warfare I was facing in my own church facilities. She was the first person to talk with me about it.

A Power Encounter

One day while in prayer the Lord spoke to me very clearly, "When you enter this building I want you to walk around the sanctuary praising Me out loud. You will circumvent the whole room clapping your hands and praising Me loudly. Do this every time you enter and every time you leave. Some days I will have you walk it several times. Do not forget, every time you come in and every time you go out, go through the auditorium and walk around it clapping and praising Me out loud, very loudly."

Week after week, I obeyed the Lord, every time I came in and every time I went out. I would walk down one outside aisle across the altar area up the other outside aisle and through the foyer, clapping my hands and loudly declaring, "Praise you Lord, Hallelujah. You are the awesome God. You are holy, Hallelujah, Hallelujah. I praise You Lord!"

One day while doing the praise walk through the foyer I heard a sneer. It was audible! I stopped; took a step backward and looked down the center aisle toward the pulpit. What I saw was unnerving. Sitting on a large throne, directly in front of, and covering, the pulpit was a huge demonic being leering at me and snarling. "This is my territory," he growled, "and you cannot have it. It rightfully belongs to me." A surge of power rose up inside of me and I shouted back, "This is the Lord's house. You will not remain here. In the name of the Lord Jesus Christ, you will be driven from this place."

That morning was the beginning of a direct power encounter with the prince demon that had been in control that local church for many years. It was also the beginning of the end for this demon's reign over that property and in that building. He had revealed himself; making his presence and his dominion vulnerable.

The battle continued for many months. Several times I led the congregation in anointing the doors and windows of the building. We went to the four corners of the property and prayed; establishing the authority of Jesus Christ. Nights of prayer and intercession were held. The victory was finally won after eighteen months of intense spiritual warfare. Over sixty people came to saving grace in the year that followed. The mighty name of Jesus Christ had prevailed and the kingdom of God was established.

Dr. Ed Murphy made an important observation.

Spiritual warfare and power encounter are not synonymous. While
we cannot have a power encounter without the broader context of
spiritual warfare, we can have spiritual warfare without power
encounter. In other words, all spiritual warfare does not imply power
encounter. Power encounter is unidimensional. Spiritual warfare is
multidimensional warfare with the flesh, the world, and evil super-
naturalism. Thus power encounter can really only exist by very
definition in the context of warfare with evil supernaturalism.[136]

A Difficult Beginning

Spiritual warfare for the Apostles had a less than auspicious beginning. In
fact, it was a complete failure. Jesus and the disciples had stayed in the
Northern Galilee region for six days after the teaching session at Caesarea
Philippi. During these days Jesus taught them about the suffering He would
face in Jerusalem and His crucifixion. Simon Peter became furious and
rebuked Jesus for believing and teaching such things. The confrontation
reached such a spiritual magnitude that Jesus had to rebuke the devil, who
was animating Peter's actions (Matthew 16:13-28).

Following that unusual and disturbing encounter, Jesus took the inner circle
of disciples, Peter, James and John, to the top of a mountain for a special
training session. During this lesson Jesus was transformed into His divine
glory, before their very eyes. Elijah and Moses appeared with Him.
Overcome with the experience, Peter and wanted to build memorials to
honor the glory of Jesus, Moses and Elijah. At the very moment Peter spoke,

the glory of God the Father appeared and He spoke to the three disciples, "This is my beloved Son, in whom I am well pleased, hear ye Him."[137] The disciples fell under the power of the awesome glory and covered their faces. Jesus touched them and raised them up for the experience and the lesson was over. These three men had seen, with their eyes, Jesus was, indeed, God come to earth in bodily form (Matthew 17:1-8).

As Jesus and the three disciples were coming down from the mountain, they were approached by a man whose son was demon possessed. "I brought him to your disciples and they could not heal him," the man lamented. Saddened by the ineptness of His disciples, Jesus cast out the demon (Matthew 17:14-18).

Later, the disciples asked Jesus privately, "Why could we not cast it out." "Because of the littleness of your faith; for truly I say to you, if you have faith as a mustard seed, you shall say to this mountain, 'move from here to there,' and it shall move; *And nothing shall be impossible to you.*"[138]

Working in the Realm of the Impossible

There is great power in those words, *"Nothing will be impossible for you!"* Jesus wanted His disciples to know without question or wavering, they did not have to stand powerless and anemic when confronted with the presence of demonic forces.

Scriptural records bear out that the disciples learned the lesson well. The Apostles exercised great authority and power in the early years of the church. The book of Acts records several occasions in which they faced sickness and demonic spirits with great power and effectiveness (Acts 2:43; 3:1-10; 5:1-12). Philip was used mightily by the Lord in a city of Samaria.

> *And the multitudes with one accord were giving attention to what was said by Philip, as they heard and saw the signs which he was performing. For {in the case of} many who had unclean spirits, they were coming out {of them} shouting with a loud voice; and many who had been paralyzed and lame were healed. And there was much rejoicing in that city.[139]*

There was no question in the mind of the Apostle Paul about the reality of spiritual warfare and the degree to which that war must be engaged by the church of Jesus Christ. He had personally been involved in the fight on many occasions. While in Paphos he confronted a Jewish sorcerer and false prophet named Bar-Jesus (Acts 13:6-12). We see in Acts 16:11-19 that he confronted a woman, in the city of Philippi, who was possessed with a spirit of divination. In Acts 19:11-20 the city of Ephesus experienced great revival and God performed miracles through the laying on of hands by the Apostle Paul. Many people experienced deliverance from demons. Those involved in witchcraft and sorcery were set free by the power of God and burned their fetishes and books.

By What Authority and Power?

The church of Jesus Christ has been given authority to displace devils, drive back the kingdom of darkness, and extend the kingdom of God. The war is great and it is violent (Matthew 11:12). The weapons of this war are not the armament used by natural kingdoms and earthly armies. They are spiritual weapons made strong and mighty through the divine power of Almighty God.

> *For though we walk in the flesh, we do not war according to the*
> *flesh, for the weapons of our warfare are not of the flesh, but divinely*
> *powerful for the destruction of fortresses. {We are} destroying*
> *speculations and every lofty thing raised up against*
>
> *the knowledge of God, and {we are} taking every thought captive to*
> *the obedience of Christ, and we are ready to punish all disobedience,*
> *whenever your obedience is complete.*[140]

On one occasion Jewish men from the city of Ephesus, who were not true disciples of Jesus Christ, tried to deal with the powers of darkness by exorcising some demons "by Jesus whom Paul preacheth" (Acts 19:13). Exorcism is not a biblical practice nor is it Christian. Although it is commonly practiced by the Roman Catholic Church.

Strictly speaking there are no exorcisms in the Bible. Use of the word, in its essential etymological meaning, forbids its employment with regard to the expulsion of demons by our Lord or His disciples. The word signifying, as it does, the casting out of evil spirits by conjurations, incantations, or religious or magical ceremonies, is singularly appropriate to describe Jewish and ethnic practice, but is in salient contrast to that of our Lord and His followers, who employed no such methods.

Among ancient and primitive peoples, exorcism depended to a great extent on the efficacy of magical formulas, commonly compounded of the names of deities, and repeated with exorcistic ritual over the bodies of those demon possessed. Power to cast out demons was regarded as existing in the words themselves, and great importance was attached to the correct recital of the right formulas and proper performance of the prescribed ritual.[141]

Exorcists were common among the Jewish community. Jesus was accused of being one of these practitioners by the religious Jewish leaders of His day (Matthew 12:27). F. F. Bruce also refers to the popularity of the Jewish exorcists in the Greco-Roman world:

> *Among practitioners of magic in the ancient times Jews enjoyed high respect, for they were believed to have especially effective spells at their command.*

> *Origen and Justin Martyr tell us the Jews were successful in this ministry only when they cast out demons in the name of the God of Abraham and Isaac and Jacob, and unsuccessful when they adjured in the name of kings, prophets, and patriarchs.*

> *The men in this story were not legitimate Jewish exorcists, however. They were spirit magicians, occult practitioners who happened to be Jews. There were after power names wherever they came from. Their successes in exorcism - and they had to have them to stay in business - had to come from demonic powers attached to their own life.[142]*

The results were disastrous for these Jewish exorcists in Ephesus.

> *But also some of the Jewish exorcists, who went from place to place, attempted to name over those who had the evil spirits the name of the Lord Jesus, saying, "I adjure you by Jesus whom Paul*

114

preaches." And seven sons of one Sceva, a Jewish chief priest, were

doing this. And the evil spirit answered and said to them, "I

recognize Jesus, and I know about Paul, but who are you?" And

the man, in whom was the evil spirit, leaped on them and subdued

all of them and overpowered them, so that they fled out of that house

naked and wounded. And this became known to all, both Jews and

Greeks, who lived in Ephesus; and fear fell upon them all and the

name of the Lord Jesus was being magnified.[143]

They were attempting to do spiritual warfare in the power of the flesh in the name of someone they knew nothing about. That will fail every time.

Wisdom and Discernment Must Be Employed

Whether it is the disciples of Jesus trying to drive out demons in the power of the flesh or the Sons of Sceva trying to drive out demons in the power of magic arts, effective dynamic spiritual warfare requires spiritual weapons empowered by Almighty God. The gates of hell will only be plundered when the church properly uses divine weapons that are Holy Spirit empowered. Wisdom and good discernment must also be employed by the spiritual warrior, if they are to see the kingdom of God advanced.

Francis Frangipane speaks to this issue in the introduction to his excellent volume, *The Three Battlegrounds*.

Jesus prepared His disciples for everything, including war. They saw
Him casting out demons. In fact, He sent them forth doing the

same. But before He sent them out, He charged them to become wise

"as **serpents***" yet innocent and harmless "***as doves***" (Matt*

10:16). This fusion of divine wisdom and Christ-like innocence is

the taproot of all spiritual victory. Indeed, we can defeat the enemy,

but wisdom must precede warfare and virtue must come before

victory. [Author's emphasis]

Point well taken! Much of the reaction within the Christian community to the very issue of dealing with the demonic has been brought on by unwise methods and less than virtuous means of ministry by men and women who, no doubt, mean well and want to bring help to those in need, but employ unwise and ineffective methods. When dealing with a demonized person, care must be given to the dignity of the person receiving ministry and correct discernment of the spirit. Wisdom, understanding and Holy Spirit discernment must be judicially exercised when doing spiritual mapping of a neighborhood, community or city.

Brash statements; presumptuous dealings; bold but unwise attacks against the enemy will bring disastrous results and may do great harm to the kingdom of righteousness. Jude, earthly brother of the Lord Jesus Christ, gave the following instructions.

> *But Michael the archangel, when he disputed with the devil and*
> *argued about the body of Moses, did not dare pronounce against*
> *him a railing judgment, but said, 'The Lord rebuke you.'*[144]

The Apostle Paul, a man so greatly used in spiritual warfare, gave instructions to the church at Ephesus that needs to be carefully heeded by every soldier of the cross of Jesus Christ. The church must not go to battle in human strength or with the counsel and strategy of the natural mind alone. The battle is not with flesh and blood, but with the forces of spiritual wickedness and the ruler of the darkness.

> *Finally, my brethren, be strong in the Lord and in the power of His might. Put on the whole armor of God, that you may be able to stand against the wiles of the devil. For we do not wrestle against flesh and blood, but against principalities, against powers, against the rulers of the darkness of this age, against spiritual hosts of wickedness in the heavenly places. Therefore, take up the whole armor of God, that you may be able to withstand in the evil day, and having done all, to stand.*[145]

All Authority in Heaven and in Earth

The church cannot afford to be inept or powerless before the forces of darkness. This is a war Jesus Christ has meant every believer to win. He has personally conquered the powers of darkness through His redemptive work (Colossians 2:14-15). All authority in heaven and in earth has been given to Him (Matthew 28:18). Through His Resurrection He now holds the keys of hell and death (Revelation 1:18). He has delegated all of that authority and power to the church.

> *And I will give unto thee the keys of the kingdom of heaven: and whatsoever thou shalt bind on earth shall be bound in heaven: and whatsoever thou shalt loose on earth shall be loosed in heaven.*[146]

The church is to employ that authority and power in building the kingdom of God around the world. Tragically, many pastors and local churches in America do not want to face the truth and the reality of spiritual warfare. The results are visible in every city of our nation. Drug dealers control the corners of school grounds and gang members control neighborhoods. Violence and crime hold cities hostage and the police and city council members feel powerless against their force. Pornography stores and gambling casinos have risen to a multi-billion dollar a year businesses. Homes are destroyed by divorce and sexual abuse. Young lives are lost in gang wars and drug overdoses. Children bear children out of wedlock.

It is time for the church to rise up again in the authority and power that God has given to her. Power to bind the strongman of darkness has been given to the church by the Lord Jesus Christ. Authority to loose people held in captivity resides within her hands. It is time for the church to push back the forces of darkness in all its forms evil. The church is to take down the gates of hell and plunder the enemy (Matthew 16:18).

The High Risk of Monasticism

The church was never meant to be a defensive force, waiting in a holy huddle for Jesus Christ to come back and rescue her from the evil forces of Satan. That is the whole concept of monastic living that arose in the fourth century A.D. "By the end of the sixth century monasticism had deep roots in the Western as well as in the Eastern sections of the church [Roman Catholic]."[147] The rise of monasticism plunged Europe into the Dark Ages as the power of the gospel and the spiritual authority of the church was stripped from the culture and communities of Europe. Spiritism and sinfulness of men's hearts were allowed to rise virtually unabated as the church hid away in cloisters and the Word of God was hidden in the darkness of Latin, away from the language and the heart of the common people. The church of Jesus Christ was guilty of the same sin as the Jewish leaders in Jesus' day. Jesus said, "You shut off the kingdom of heaven from men; for you do not enter in yourselves, nor do you allow those who are entering to go in."[148]

The church in America has become guilty of the same sin in the last sixty years. The Evangelical and the Pentecostal churches went monastic in two new forms. They deserted the urban centers and moved to the suburbs of the cities and they became highly program- centered to entertain the people and for radio and television broadcasts.

The results of this monastic move have produced a highly educated, well administered, and very polished and sophisticated Christian business. The church has foolishly believed that thousands in attendance and million-dollar church plants validate the authenticity and the effectiveness of their "ministry." Does that hold up under the examination of biblical principles and the mandate of the Great Commission?

While the church of Jesus Christ has busied herself within the four walls of her million dollar structures and gaudily displayed herself on television sets, American cities have plunged into depths of darkness never known in the history of the United States. Illiteracy has skyrocketed and the arts of our culture have become vulgar and distorted.

Statistics clearly show how the monastic Evangelical and Pentecostal churches in America have failed the culture and the cities of our generation, just as the monastic Roman Catholic Church failed the European culture. George Barna research shows the American culture has progressively grown darker and the church less effective and irrelevant in this generation.

The magnitude of the church's failure to impact the nation is seen in an even greater degree in a 1994 survey taken by the Barna Group among teenagers who attended Evangelical and Pentecostal churches in America (3,795 teenagers from thirteen denominations, 86% claimed salvation by faith in Jesus Christ) and reported by Josh McDowell and Bob Hostetler. The following are samples from that survey.

16% had participated in sexual intercourse

45% would be likely to have intercourse with a person they believed they loved if the opportunity presented itself.

66% had lied to their parent or teacher in the last three months.

29% believed there is no such thing as an absolute truth.

17% did not believe the Bible provides a standard for living.

48% believe matters of morals and ethics, truth means different things to different people; no one can be absolutely positive that they have the truth.[149]

The moral landslide of America can be placed squarely at the feet of the church of Jesus Christ who has failed to effectively do spiritual warfare. Instead of driving back the forces of darkness and plundering the gates of hell, the church has begun to deny their existence and gladly welcomed the cohabitation of demonic spirits and the doctrine of devils.

*Now the Spirit expressly says that in latter times some will depart
from the faith, giving heed to deceiving spirits and doctrines of
demons.[150]*

This attitude and spiritual climate must be changed if America is to be saved.

Crashing the Gates of Hell

There is hope for America. Many pastors and churches are awakening to the responsibility given by the Lord Jesus Christ. They are rising up in the power and authority He has given to do exploits in His name. They are taking on the gates of hell in their neighborhoods and cities. They are seeing new dimensions of the kingdom God and souls are being set free. In every case where this is happening three important principles have been discovered and employed by the church.

The first principle is that the church understands the nature of the conflict. There are three dimensions to the spiritual war the church is fighting. The conflict within personal lives to live victoriously over sin, temptation and the devil (putting on the armor of God), the conflict to save souls from the prisons of darkness and the power of sin, and the conflict to extend the kingdom of God into regions and territories of the earth. The second principle is that the church accepts personal responsibility: for their families', friends', and neighbors' salvation; for their neighborhoods', communities' and cities' deliverance from sin, darkness and evil; and for revival in their state and nation. The third principle is that the church learns to effectively use the weapons God has given to her for this warfare.

Spiritual Armament

The first two points will be dealt with in separate chapters. What are the weapons of war that must be carefully studied and employed by the soldiers of God's kingdom? The Apostle Paul said, "Lest Satan should get an advantage of us: for we are not ignorant of his devices" (2 Corinthians 2:11 KJV). The church must not be ignorant of Satan's devices nor should she be ignorant of the mighty weapons God has placed in her arsenal for advancement against the kingdom of darkness. If earthly armies take great effort to carefully train and even retrain their men and women in the proficient use of weapons and military armor to protect their nations against belligerence; how much more should the church be training the saints in the use of divine weaponry for the deliverance of the souls of mankind, and the protection of our cities and nation from the powers of darkness.

Six mighty weapons have been given to the church to use in this spiritual war against Satan and his kingdom: the mighty name of Jesus Christ, the mighty power of praise and worship, the mighty power of prayer and fasting, the overcoming power of the blood of the Lamb, the conquering power of their testimony, and the victorious power of their faith.

It must be clearly understood these weapons are spiritual armaments to be used in the power and dynamic of the Holy Spirit. They are not to be employed in the energy of the soul or the strength of the flesh. Rick Godwin says,

> *You may be 'God's Rambo,' taking on the powers of hell,*
> *exercising the authority of Jesus, but unless you have the right*
> *weapons, it is an exercise in futility.*[151]

The Apostle urged the church at Corinth, "Though we walk in the flesh, we do not war after the flesh: For the weapons of our warfare are not carnal but mighty through God, to the pulling down of strongholds" (2 Corinthians 10:3-4). The believer's weapons are "*mighty through God.*" They are not mighty through how loud one prays, sings or shouts. They are not powerful against the enemy forces because of the commanding presence of a person. Demons do not leave or give up territory because of the dynamic way a person may minister.

The Weapon That Brings the Enemy to His Knees

The first weapon with which the believer must become proficient is the mighty name of Jesus Christ. Jesus said Mark 16:17, "In my name they shall cast out devils". In Luke 10:17 the seventy disciples said, "Lord even demons are subject to us in your name". The Apostle Peter said to the lame man, "In the name of Jesus Christ of Nazareth, walk" (Acts 3:6). The Apostle Paul said to the woman with a spirit of divination, "In the name of Jesus Christ, I command you to come out of her." Jesus said, "Whatsoever, ye shall ask in my name, that will I do that the Father maybe glorified in the Son. If ye ask anything in my name, *I will do it* (John 14:13-14) ... That whatsoever ye ask of the Father in my name, He may give it you (John 15:16) ... And in that day ye shall ask Me nothing. Verily, verily, I say unto you, whatsoever ye shall ask the Father in My name, *He will give it you.* Hitherto have ye asked nothing in My name: *ask, and ye shall receive*, that your joy may be full. These things have I spoken unto you in proverbs: but the time cometh, when I shall no more speak unto you in proverbs, but I shall shew you plainly of the Father. At that day *ye shall ask in My name*: and I say not unto you, that I will pray the Father for you" (John 16:23-26). [emphasis mine]

Speaking in the name of Jesus Christ is using the authority of His name. His name is above all other names (Philemon 3:9-10). His name has all power and authority in heaven and in earth (Matthew 28:18). He is the head of all principalities and powers (Colossians 2:9-10). He is above all rule, dominion, principalities and powers and all things have been put under His feet (Ephesians 1:20-23). When a child of God prays and takes authority in the name of Jesus Christ, all of the authority in His name comes to bear in that situation or circumstance. All entities and all forces of darkness at work in that situation or circumstance come under the authority and power of that name. They must submit. They must yield. They must surrender.

Wesley Duewel gives six roles the name of Jesus has in a person's prayer.

> *1. The name of Jesus gives instant access to God's throne. The authority of the name unlocks heaven's door.*

> *2. The name identifies you with who Jesus is. There are said to be 143 names and titles given to Jesus in the Bible. Each is another ray of God's light illuminating who Jesus is and what He does.*

> *3. The name of Jesus sanctifies your prayer. You can pray no unworthy prayer in His name. Any prayer that is selfish, vindictive, or with wrong motive dies on your lips when you take His name... His holy name is a flaming fire that consumes all that is unworthy in His sight and contrary to His will. Unworthy prayer cannot penetrate to Christ's intercessory throne.*

124

4. The Name unites with His will. You cannot ask in Jesus'
name what is contrary to His will, what Jesus would not
ask if He were praying.

5. The Name gives you His authority. When you ask in His
name, you come as His representative, you come for His
sake - not for your own sake. . .. Heaven's authority
backs any prayer that you truly pray in Jesus' name - not
because you use those words but because you and the
prayer are truly in His name.

6. The Name gives Jesus' endorsement. Jesus is the amen of all
prayer prayed in the Spirit.[152]

Dr. Duewel continues:

There are many militant uses of the name of Jesus. This list is only
suggestive…In the light of the role of the name, use the name again
and again to the glory of God and to the advancement of His
Kingdom.

Use the name to clear the spiritual atmosphere...

1. Use the name to claim protection...

2. Use the name to express your longing.

3. Use the name to enforce the honor of Christ.

4. Use the name of Jesus in militant faith.

125

5. Use the name in holy determination.

6. Use the name in the command of faith.[153]

The Weapon That Chains the Enemy

The second mighty weapon in the believer's arsenal is the power of praise and worship. Bill Subritzky says,

> *Another wonderful method of deliverance is praising God. I will often ask the person being delivered to simply say the words, 'Praise God.' They may say it up to fifty times before the demons scream and say they won't praise God, but then we know we have the victory and as the person presses on they are set free.*

> *We know, of course, the reason for all this, namely that God lives in the praises of His people, and as we praise God the Spirit of God comes down and drives out the demon power.*

> *'But you are holy, Who inhabit the praises of Israel.' (Psalm 22:3)*[154]

This is clearly borne out in Scripture. The Old Testament and the New Testament have occasions when the enemy of God was defeated through the praise and worship of the saints. Joshua and Israel conquered the walled city of Jericho through praise and worship (Joshua 6:1-21). Jehoshaphat and the armies of Israel won a great victory over a coalition army of their enemies by placing the worshippers out front to lead the warriors into battle (2 Chronicles 20:1-27). Paul and Silas were released from the prison in Philippi

126

when God unlocked the prison door and loosed their chains in response to their praise and worship (Acts 16:25-28).

The Psalmist wrote:

> *Let the godly ones exult in glory; let them sing for joy on their beds.*
> *{Let} the high praises of God {be} in their mouth, and a two-*
> *edged sword in their hand, To execute vengeance on the nations, and*
> *punishment on the peoples; To bind their kings with chains, and*
> *their nobles with fetters of iron; To execute on them the judgment*
> *written; this is an honor for all His godly ones. Praise the LORD!*[155]

Even the praise and worship of children can be a mighty weapon against the powers of darkness. King David wrote in Psalm 8 the following verses.

> *O LORD, our Lord, How majestic is Thy name in all the earth,*
> *Who hast displayed Thy splendor above the heavens! From the*
> *mouth of infants and nursing babes Thou hast established strength,*
> *Because of Thine adversaries, To make the enemy and the revengeful*
> *cease.* [156]

The New International Version translates verse two, "From the lips of children and infants you have ordained praise because of your enemies, to silence the foe and the avenger." Gesenius defines the Hebrew word *oz*, translated as "strength" in the KJV and the NAS, not only as strength and might but as *"splendor, majesty glory and praise* (Psalm 8:3; 29:1; 68:35; 99:4; Exodus 15:2; 2 Chronicles 30:21), 'Instruments of praise,' employed in praising God."[157] Harris, Archer and Waltke state the following, "Dahood translates this word [*oz*] three times as 'praise' (Psalm 29:1; 68:34 and 96:7). Note the LXX and NT use of 'praise' in Psalm 8:2 and Matthew 21:6."[158]

The Weapon That Breaks the Yoke

The third mighty weapon employed by the church is prayer and fasting. Jesus taught the disciples, "Howbeit, this kind goeth not out but by prayer and fasting" (Matthew 17:21).

> *Full-souled seeking of God by prayer with fasting enables God to do things in answer to prayer that He cannot do without the level of praying that is reached by the added fasting. God has ordained that fasting help release His power to work in a more decisive and sometimes more immediate way. We therefore have a very sacred responsibility to fast.*[159]

There are strongholds of the enemy that cannot be torn down and demonic forces that cannot be driven out of lives except by the prevailing prayer of a heart that is humbled through fasting.

> *'Is this not the fast which I choose, To loosen the bonds of wickedness, To undo the bands of the yoke, And to let the oppressed go free, And break every yoke? 'Is it not to divide your bread with the hungry, And bring the homeless poor into the house; When you see the naked, to cover him; And not to hide yourself from your own flesh? 'Then your light will break out like the dawn, And your recovery will speedily spring forth; And your righteousness will go before you; The glory of the LORD will be your rear guard.*

'Then you will call, and the LORD will answer; You will cry, and
He will say, 'Here I am.' If you remove the yoke from your midst,
The pointing of the finger, and speaking wickedness, And if you
give yourself to the hungry, And satisfy the desire of the afflicted,
Then your light will rise in darkness, And your gloom will become
like midday. 'And the LORD will continually guide you, And
satisfy your desire in scorched places, And give strength to your
bones; And you will be like a watered garden, And like a spring of
water whose waters do not fail. 'And those from among you will
rebuild the ancient ruins; You will raise up the age-old foundations;
And you will be called the repairer of the breach, The restorer of the
streets in which to dwell.' [160]

The power of this mighty weapon can break the yoke off our children and set
the oppressed around us free. The streets of our cities can become safe again
and we can see the ruin of our cities rebuilt.

The Overcoming Weapon

The fourth mighty weapon against the kingdom of darkness is the blood of
the lamb. The Apostle John watched in amazement as God revealed to Him
the great defeat of Satan and his hellish hosts.

And there was war in heaven: Michael and his angels fought
against the dragon; and the dragon fought and his angels, And
prevailed not; neither was their place found any more in heaven.
And the great dragon was cast out, that old serpent, called the
Devil, and Satan, which deceiveth the whole world: he was cast out

into the earth, and his angels were cast out with him. And I heard
a loud voice saying in heaven, Now is come salvation, and strength,
and the kingdom of our God, and the power of his Christ: for the
accuser of our brethren is cast down, which accused them before our
God day and night. **And they overcame him by the blood**
of the Lamb, *and by the word of their testimony; and they loved*
not their lives unto the death. Therefore, rejoice, ye heavens, and ye
that dwell in them. Woe to the inhabiters of the earth and of the
sea! For the devil is come down unto you, having great wrath,
because he knoweth that he hath but a short time.[161] *[emphasis*
mine]

The Apostle Paul said it is the blood of Jesus Christ that delivers a person from the powers of darkness and into the kingdom of God's dear Son (Colossians 1:13-14). It is the blood of Jesus Christ that justifies a person and purges a soul from dead works to serve the living God (Romans 3:25, 5:9; Ephesians 1:7; Hebrews 9:14). It is the blood of Jesus Christ that bought the church (Acts 20:28; Revelation 5:9). It is through the blood of Jesus Christ that God has made peace (Colossians 1:20). It is by the blood of Jesus Christ a person can come into the very holy presence of Almighty God (Hebrews 10:19). It is the blood of Jesus Christ that makes a person holy (Hebrews 13:12). It is through the blood of Jesus Christ that mankind has been redeemed from the slave market of sin and Satan, never to go back into slavery again (Romans 3:24; 1 Peter. 1:19). It is by the blood of Jesus Christ that one can have fellowship with God (1 John 1:7).

It was by the blood of the Passover lamb, painted on the door posts of their house that Israel was delivered from the power of the death angel moving through Egypt, killing all of the first born. It is the blood of the eternal Passover Lamb, Jesus Christ, that mankind is delivered from the power and authority of Satan, the one who had the power of death (John 1:29, 36; 1 Peter 1:19; Hebrews 2:14; Revelation 5:6-13; 7:14).

J. O. Fraser, pioneer missionary to the Lisu tribe in Southwest China with the China Inland Mission, experienced how intense the wrestling with the powers of darkness can be before the 'strong man' is finally forced to yield up his prey.

'What it showed me was that deliverance from the power of the evil one comes through definite resistance on the ground of the cross. Definite resistance on the ground of the cross was what brought me light. For I found that it worked...'

The redemptive purposes of God move to their fruition by incarnation. So today, the same principle applies. God has chosen us for the present as well as for the future. We are chosen for 'good works that God hath before ordained that we should walk in them.' And part of that has to be in activities that bring us into close touch with His enemy. One of the main purposes in the incarnation of Jesus Christ was to 'render powerless him that had the power of death, that is, the devil' (Hebrews 12:14). The only way the devil can be rendered powerless today is as the truth and reality of the Savior's victory through His death on the cross is administered by the believer on earth operating in the name of the Lord Jesus Christ.[162]

The Weapon of Declaration

The fifth mighty weapon Jesus Christ has given to the church is the conquering power of their testimony. "And they overcome him by the blood of the lamb, and by the word of their testimony" (Revelation 12:11). Dr. Neil Anderson declares, "Before you can truly be free... you need to know who you are in Christ."[163]

A believer's testimony is a faith declaration of the truths of God's Word and the efficacious power of its working in their life. It is an important declaration of three things.

1. Belief in Jesus Christ; who He is (God in the flesh); His nature (In Him dwells all the fullness of the Godhead bodily); His character; His Word (John 1:1-14; Colossians 2:9-10; Hebrews 4:13, 13:8;1 John 1:1-9, 4:1-11).

2. Salvation through faith in Jesus Christ and His death, burial and resurrection (Romans 6:1-14) and their position in Jesus Christ and His resurrection (Romans 6:1-14; Ephesians 2:6; Colossians 3:3; 2 Peter 1:2-4).

3. Complete victory in Jesus Christ over all powers of darkness (Luke 10:19: Romans 8:31-39; Colossians 2:12-15; Hebrews 2:14; James 4:6-7; 1 Peter 5:6-9)

The Believer's Weapon of Victory

The weapons God has given to the church are mighty and they are powerful against all the plans, schemes and attacks of the enemy. The power of these weapons is realized by faith. The Apostle John said, "For whatsoever is born of God overcometh the world: and this is the victory that overcometh the world, even our faith" (1 John 5:4). The writer of Hebrews declared faith to be that which enabled the victorious men and women of history overcome every obstacle they faced. "By faith Able offered to God a better sacrifice…By faith Enoch was taken up…By faith Noah… prepared an ark…By faith Abraham, when he was called, obeyed…By faith Abraham, when he was tested, offered up Isaac…By faith Isaac blessed Jacob and Esau…By faith Jacob… blessed each of the son of Joseph…By faith Joseph… gave orders concerning his bones…By faith Moses… was hidden… by his parents…By faith Moses, when he had grown up refused to be called the son of Pharaoh's daughter… By faith he left Egypt… By faith he kept the Passover and the sprinkling of the blood… By faith they passed through the Red Sea…By faith the walls of Jericho fell down…By faith Rahab the harlot did not perish…By faith [Gideon, Barak, Samson, Jephthah, David, Samuel, the prophets] conquered kingdoms, performed acts of righteousness, obtained promises, shut the mouths of lions, quenched the power of fire, escaped the edge of the sword, from weakness were made strong, became mighty in war, put foreign armies to flight. Women received back their dead by resurrection" (Hebrews 11:4-35).

The blessed man of faith George Muller gives the following account in his autobiography.

> *It pleased the Lord, I think, to give me in such cases something like the gift (not grace) of faith, so that unconditionally I could ask and look for an answer. The difference between the gift and the grace of faith seems to me this. According to the gift of faith, I am able to do*

133

a thing, or believe that a thing will come to pass, the not doing of

which, or the not believing of which, would not be sin; according to

the grace of faith, I am able to do a thing, or believe that a thing

will come to pass, respecting which I have the word of God as the

ground to rest upon, and, therefore, the not doing it, or not to believe

it, would be sin.[164]

Mr. Muller's walk of faith became renowned, as he ministered the word of life, led an orphanage, and supplied many needs for missionaries around the world. All of this done by faith. The years 1859-1860, recorded $350,000.00 was the audited income into his ministry, without once asking for an offering. The funds were received by faith alone.

It is absolutely clear that our lack of faith limits God's freedom of

working mightily. It stopped Jesus from using His miracle-working

power (Mark 6:5). From the standpoint of omnipotence, God is

almighty - His power is utterly unlimited. From the standpoint of

His sovereignty, God can do what He will. But from the standpoint

of His grace, He has chosen normally to limit His miracle answers

to our believing. 'According to your faith' (Matthew 9:29), Jesus

said.[165]

Faith is having absolute confidence and total reliance upon God's nature, character and infallible Word. That is the victory that overcomes the world and the kingdom of darkness.

He who dwells in the shelter of the Most High Will abide in the

shadow of the Almighty. I will say to the LORD, "My refuge and my fortress, My God, in whom I trust!" For it is He who delivers you from the snare of the trapper, And from the deadly pestilence. He will cover you with His pinions, And under His wings you may seek refuge; His faithfulness is a shield and bulwark. You will not be afraid of the terror by night, or of the arrow that flies by day; Of the pestilence that stalks in darkness, Or of the destruction that lays waste at noon. A thousand may fall at your side, And ten thousand at your right hand; But it shall not approach you. You will only look on with your eyes, And see the recompense of the wicked. For you have made the LORD, my refuge, Even the Most High, your dwelling place. No evil will befall you, Nor will any plague come near your tent. For He will give His angels charge concerning you, To guard you in all your ways. They will bear you up in their hands, Lest you strike your foot against a stone. You will tread upon the lion and cobra, The young lion and the serpent you will trample down. Because he has loved Me, therefore I will deliver him; I will set him securely on high, because he has known My name. He will call upon Me, and I will answer him; I will be with him in trouble; I will rescue him, and honor him. With a long life I will satisfy him, and let him behold My salvation.[166]

A New Species of Mankind

My dear Wormwood,

I have been in correspondence with Slumtrimpet who is in charge of your patient's young woman, and begin to see the chink in her armour. It is an unobtrusive little vice which she shares with nearly all women who have grown up in an intelligent circle united by a clearly defined belief; and it consists in a quite untroubled assumption that the outsiders who do not share this belief are really too stupid and ridiculous. The males, who habitually meet these outsiders, do not feel that way; their confidence, if they are confident, is of a different kind. Hers, which she supposed to be due to Faith, is in reality largely due to the mere colour she has taken from her surroundings. . . .. Now the element of ignorance and naiveté' in all this is so large, and the element of spiritual pride so small, that it gives us little hope for the girl herself. But have you thought of how it can be made to influence your won patient?

Your affectionate Uncle,

Screwtape

Lewis, The Screwtape Letters

The words came piercing into my spirit like an arrow from heaven, "Your past and your present circumstances do not have to determine your future or your identity. Jesus Christ has made it possible for you to live victorious in every area of your life." I had known that truth for several years. But that day, as I was on my way to speak at a drug and alcohol recovery center, it came with fresh power. I had been wrestling with what words to share with these men and women looking for a new lease on life. "Jesus, what do you want to speak to these dear ones?" As I waited on Him, the Holy Spirit brought those words resounding into my spirit. *"Your past or your present circumstances do not*

137

have to determine your future or your identity." That is the hope every person can have when their life is hidden *in Jesus Christ.*

Therefore, Walk in Newness of Life

He had made the wonderful discovery of salvation by faith, several years before. Yet, there were areas in his life where the resurrection power of Jesus Christ had not penetrated. They were areas that seemed almost impossible to change, although he had tried several times. He was what I like to call a spiritual P.O.W. (prisoner of war). "Can I ever be free," he asked me over lunch. The answer is absolute, "Yes!" I shared with him many of the following principles for living a victorious and overcoming Christian life. Jesus declared, "If, therefore, the Son shall make you free, you shall be free indeed."[167]

The Apostle Paul made an astounding statement in Romans 6:14. "Sin shall not have dominion over you, for you are not under law but under grace." The completed work of Jesus Christ makes it possible for everyone, who desires, to live free from negative attitudes, stifling emotions, unbreakable habits, life controlling phobias, or generational strongholds. All of these life debilitating circumstances and more are related to satanic strongholds, unless there is a disease or physical disorder that is a contributing factor. In that case, a doctor should be consulted along with the spiritual ministry.

Every person will face conflict in four areas of their life: the self-man (that is the will), the thought life (conscious and subconscious areas of the mind), the emotions (the feeling center of life, i.e. anger, resentment, happy), and the

138

flesh (natural and unnatural appetites that are aroused through the five senses of the human body). Spiritual victory must be won in these four areas if consistent healthy living is to take place. The Apostle Paul said, "Let not sin reign in your mortal bodies that ye should obey it in the lust thereof (Romans 6:12). Through the resurrection power of the Holy Spirit each of these areas can be overcome.

> *But if the Spirit of Him who raised Jesus from the dead dwells in you, He who raised Christ from the dead will also give life to your mortal bodies through His Spirit who dwells in you. Therefore, brethren, we are debtors--not to the flesh, to live according to the flesh. For if you live according to the flesh you will die; but if by the Spirit you put to death the deeds of the body, you will live. For as many as are led by the Spirit of God, these are sons of God. [168]*

Watchman Nee gives this solemn warning in his exhaustive volume *The Spiritual Man.*

> *The Christian's spirit can be influenced by either of two forces: The Holy Spirit or the evil spirit. He commits a fatal blunder who thinks his spirit can be controlled solely by the Holy Spirit and not be so by the evil spirit too. Let it be forever known that aside from the Spirit that is from God, there is additionally, "the spirit of the world" (1 Corinthians 2:12), which is in fact the spiritual foe of Ephesians 6:12. Except the Christian shuts up his spirit to resist, he may find the evil one usurping his spirit through deceit and counterfeit.[169]*

The Apostle Paul urged the church at Ephesus to grow to the full stature of spiritual maturity in Jesus Christ, so they would not easily be tossed to and fro by the spirits of deceit and unscrupulous men. Living a victorious and overcoming spiritual life requires maturity and growth in four ways. The foundation of a healthy and overcoming life starts with becoming a new creature in Jesus Christ. They must learn who they are *in Christ* and how to apply the principles of Romans chapters six and eight. Proficiency with the whole armor of God and effective spiritual warfare must be learned and consistent Spirit-filled living must become a passion and a way of life.

The Foundation for Healthy Living

Jesus said, "The thief comes but for to steal, to kill and to destroy. But, I have come that you might have life and that more abundantly." God's will for his children has always been abundant living. Addictions; profanity, stealing, abuse, low self-worth; worry, anxiety, hatred are afflictions from the enemy of mankind who seeks "to steal, kill and destroy" (John 10:10). The good news of the Gospel of Jesus Christ is every human being, who wishes, can be set free through the regenerating power of Holy Spirit.

The Apostle Paul declared, "Therefore, if any man be in Christ, he is a new creature: Old things are passed away, behold; all things are become new" (2 Corinthians 5:17). The amazing miracle of new birth in Jesus Christ is two-fold. The first part of the miracle is total removal of all the sins the person has ever committed and the judgment for doing them. The second part of the miracle is the impartation of a brand new life source. That is why the Apostle Paul called them a "new creature." Dr. Thayer defines the Greek word for creature (Strong's number NT 2937) as follows. "ktisis--the act of founding, establishing, building, etc. a) the act of creating, creation, b) creation, that is, a thing created; used of individual things, beings, a creature, a creation: 1) anything created, 2) after a rabbinical usage (by which a man converted from idolatry to Judaism   was called), 3) the sum or aggregate of things created, c) an institution, an ordinance170

Literally, in Jesus Christ, a person who has been born again is a new creation. "Not by works of righteousness which we have done, but according to His mercy He saved us, by the washing of regeneration, and renewing of the Holy Ghost" (Titus 3:5).

The Apostle Peter describes the experience as receiving a divine life source. "Whereby are given unto us exceeding great and precious promises, that by these ye might be partakers of the divine nature having escaped the corruption that is in the world through lust" (2 Peter 1:4).

Again, we refer to Dr. Thayer, for the meaning of divine nature.

> *Divine (Strong's number NT 2304) theios,*
> *a) a general name of deities or divinities as used by the Greeks,*
> *b) spoken of the only and true God, the trinity:*
> > *1) used of Christ,*
> > *2) the Holy Spirit,*
> > *3) the Father,*
> *Nature (Strong's NT 5449) phusis, nature:*
> > *a) the nature of things, the force, laws, order of nature:*
> > > *1) as opposed to what is monstrous, abnormal, perverse,*

2) as opposed what has been produced by the
art of man: the natural branches, that is,
branches by the operation of nature,
3) birth, physical origin
4) a mode of feeling and acting which by long
habit, has become nature,
5) the sum of innate properties and powers by which one
person differs from others, distinctive native peculiarities,
natural characteristics: the natural strength, ferocity, and
intractability of beasts 171

Kenneth Wuest gives great clarification to this passage of Scripture.

Through these promises, the saints have become partakers of,
sharers in the divine nature. Peter is here referring to regeneration as
in I Peter 1:23. This divine nature implanted in the inner being of
the believing sinner, becomes the source of his new life and actions.
By its energy in giving him both the desire and the power to do
God's will, he has escaped the corruption that is in the world.[172]

When a person is born again, God places within him the Holy Spirit, to be
the source of a whole new life. A life filled with abundant living. This was
God's creative purposes and design for mankind, from the beginning. God
spoke to Adam and Eve, "Be fruitful and multiply... " (Genesis 1:28), and
God blessed Noah and his sons, and said unto them, Be fruitful, and multiply,
and replenish the earth" (Genesis 9:1 KJV). God promised Abraham to make
him a great nation, to make his name great and to bless him (Genesis 12:2).

Jacob wrestled with the Lord until He promised to bless him (Genesis 32:22-32).

God promised Israel, "And it shall come to pass, if thou shalt hearken diligently unto the voice of the LORD thy God, to observe and to do all His commandments which I command thee this day, that the LORD thy God will set thee on high above all nations of the earth: And all these blessings shall come on thee, and overtake thee, if thou shalt hearken unto the voice of the LORD thy God.[173]

God has not changed His mind. It is only the sin of man's heart that keeps him from living the abundant life for which God created him. Everyone who receives Jesus Christ as Lord and Savior receives the source of abundant life and all the blessings God has stored up in heaven.

> *Blessed be the God and Father of our Lord Jesus Christ, who hath blessed us with all spiritual blessings in heavenly places in Christ: According as He hath chosen us in Him before the foundation of the world, that we should be holy and without blame before Him in love: Having predestinated us unto the adoption of children by Jesus Christ to Himself, according to the good pleasure of His will, to the praise of the glory of His grace, wherein He hath made us accepted in the beloved. In whom we have redemption through His blood, the forgiveness of sins, according to the riches of His grace.[174]*

The Romans 6 Principle

The Apostle Paul asked a very probing question in his letter to the church in

Rome. "What shall I say then, shall I continue in sin, that grace may abound" (Romans 6:1)? The apostle is pointedly asking, should those who have been born again continue to live bound by habits and behavior patterns of their previous sinful life? His answer was a resounding, "God forbid!

"How shall we that are dead to sin, live any long therein" (Romans 6:2)? Paul affirms the believer's victory because of their position in Jesus Christ. "Do you not know that all of us who have been baptized into Christ Jesus have been baptized into His death" (Romans 6:3)? "A true knowledge of God and our identity in Christ is the greatest determinant of our mental health. A false concept of God and the misplaced deification of Satan are the greatest contributors to mental illness."[175]

Six principles are given in Romans chapter six and chapter eight that are vital to the victorious life of every child of God. Watchman Nee says, "Romans 6 lays the foundation for the Christian's deliverance from sin. Such deliverance God provides for every believer; all may enter."[176]

Sin does not have dominion over a child of God because their life of sin was crucified and buried with Jesus Christ, to never live again (Romans 6:3, 6-7). When Jesus Christ was hanging on the cross of Calvary, the sins of every person were nailed to that cross with Him. "He Himself bore our sins in His body on the cross, that we might die to sin and live to righteousness" (1 Peter 2:24 NAS). When Jesus Christ was buried in the tomb the sins of mankind were buried with Him never to live again.

> *Therefore, we have been buried with Him through baptism into death, in order that as Christ was raised from the dead through the glory of the Father, so we too might walk in newness of life. For if*

we have become united with Him in the likeness of His death,

certainly we shall be also in the likeness of His resurrection,

knowing this, that our old self was crucified with Him, that our

body of sin might be done away with, that we should no longer be

slaves to sin; for he who has died is freed from sin.[177]

A child of God does not have to let sin reign over their life because they have been raised to new life in Jesus Christ.

Therefore, we have been buried with Him through baptism into

death, in order that as Christ was raised from the dead through the

glory of the Father, so we too might walk in newness of life. For if

we have become united with Him in the likeness of His death,

certainly we shall be also in the likeness of His resurrection.[178]

The Apostle Paul urged the Romans believers, "Even so, consider yourselves to be dead to sin but alive to God in Jesus Christ" (Romans 6:11). Every child of God has resurrection life within them by the Holy Spirit who dwells in their heart (Romans 8:11). The born again child of God is no longer obligated to live by the old behavior patterns; the old attitudes; the old life styles and the old habits. They have a new life source and a new power living within them that will enable them to develop new behavior patterns; new attitudes; new life style and break the old habits and addictions. That is why Paul urged the Roman believers, "Therefore do not let sin reign in your mortal body that you should obey its lusts, and do not go on presenting the members of your body to sin as instruments of unrighteousness; but present yourselves to God as those alive from the dead, and your members as instruments of righteousness to God" (Romans 6:12-13). The body members once used to commit acts of sin can now be used as mighty weapons of righteousness to bless where they once cursed; to love where they once hated; to bring peace where they once brought anger and violence; to give kindness where they once gave revenge; to bring honor and respect where they once brought immorality.

The Child of God does not have to live with continual thoughts and feelings of condemnation and accusations or with the shame and humiliation of those things they have done wrong. "There is therefore, now, no condemnation to them which are in Christ Jesus, who walk not after the flesh but after the Spirit" (Romans 8:1). Every person who asks Jesus Christ to forgive their sin and come live in their heart has the wonderful joy of living free from the condemnation and shame of their past life. How can that be? The Apostle Paul said, "For the law of the Spirit of life in Christ Jesus has set you free from the law of sin and of death" (Romans 8:2). The sacrifice of Jesus Christ paid the price for our sin and His resurrection made it possible for us to live in the power of resurrection life. When He sprinkled His own blood on the mercy seat of heaven, He made it possible for every person to be justified before Almighty God. "But God demonstrates His own love toward us, in that while we were yet sinners, Christ died for us. Much more then, having now been justified by His blood, we shall be saved from the wrath of God through Him."[179] Justification is the judicial action taken by Almighty God in which He made a divine fiat, declaring all who receive Jesus Christ to be just as if they had never sinned and making the person holy. The sin is removed never to be remembered against them again (Hebrews 10:15-17), and they are declared to be the righteousness of Jesus Christ, holy as He is holy (2 Corinthians 5:21).

146

Every person that receives Jesus Christ as Lord and Savior is filled with the Holy Spirit and resurrection life. They are also raised up and seated with Christ in heavenly places (Ephesians 2:6). That is, they are spiritually sitting with Christ in the realm and power of His kingdom.

> *Giving thanks to the Father, who has qualified us to share in the inheritance of the saints in light. For He delivered us from the domain of darkness, and transferred us to the kingdom of His Beloved Son, in whom we have redemption, the forgiveness of sins.*[180]

Seated with Christ, the believers are in the place to receive the full blessings God has stored up for them "in heavenly places" (Ephesians 1:3). They are also in a place of great protection that can never be defeated or conquered by their enemies.

> *What then shall we say to these things? If God is for us, who is against us? He who did not spare His own Son, but delivered Him up for us all, how will He not also with Him freely give us all things? Who will bring a charge against God's elect? God is the one who*

> *justifies; who is the one who condemns? Christ Jesus is He who died, yes, rather who was raised, who is at the right hand of God, who also intercedes for us. Who shall separate us from the love of Christ? Shall tribulation, or distress, or persecution, or famine, or nakedness, or peril, or sword? Just as it is written "For Thy sake we are being put to death all day long; We were considered as sheep to be slaughtered." But in all these things we overwhelmingly conquer through Him who loved us. For I am convinced that neither death, nor life, nor angels, nor principalities, nor things present, nor*

147

things to come, nor powers, nor height, nor depth, nor any other
created thing, shall be able to separate us from the love of God,
which is in Christ Jesus our Lord.[181]

The believer's freedom from accusation and condemnation; hope of victory over old habits; assurance of abundant living and eternal life have been made certain because of who they are *in* Jesus Christ. Notice the Scripture repeats the words "in Christ" time and again. The following are a few of the references: "Baptized into Christ" (Romans 63); "Alive to God in Christ" (Romans 6:11); "No condemnation... in Christ" (Romans 8:1); "Law of the Spirit of life in Christ" (Romans 8:2); "Cannot separate us from the love... which is in Christ" (Romans 8:39); "In Christ he is a new creature" (2 Corinthians 5:17); "In Christ reconciling the world to Himself" (2 Corinthians 5:19); "That we might become the righteousness of God in Him" (2 Corinthians 5:21); "Blessed us with every spiritual blessing... in Christ" (Ephesians 1:3); "He chose us in Him before the foundation of the world" (Ephesians 1:4); "His grace which He freely bestowed on us in the Beloved" (Ephesians 1:6); "In Him we have redemption" (Ephesians 1:7); "In Him... obtained and inheritance" (Ephesians 1:11); "Ye were sealed in Him with the Holy Spirit" (Eph. 1:13); "Seated us with Him in heavenly places in Christ" (Ephesians 2:6); "His grace in kindness toward us in Christ" (Ephesians 1:7); "Created in Christ Jesus for good works" (Ephesians 2:10); "We have boldness and confident access... in Him" (Ephesians 3:12).

The Scriptures also refers to the believer being "with Him" and "united with Him." The believer is "buried with Him by baptism" (Romans 6:4). The believer's "old man is crucified with Him". (Romans 6:6) The believer's old life of sin is "dead with Christ... That shall also live with Him". (Romans 6:8).

148

The believer is "joint-heirs with Christ" and they shall also be "glorified together" (Romans 8:17). Father shall "with Him also freely give us all things" (Romans 8:32).

Nothing shall be able to "separate us from the love of God, which is in Christ Jesus our Lord" (Rom. 8:39).

> *When I was a new believer, struggling to find victory in my Christian life, I heard the late Dr. J. Vernon McGee, then pastor of the Church of the Open Door in Los Angeles, preach on this text (Romans 8:1-4). The details of what he taught I have forgotten, but I have never forgotten the impact of that sermon on my life and one phrase he continually repeated. 'The most important word in the New Testament for the believer is the preposition in, in Christ and in the spirit,' McGee affirmed. This truth came to my parched heart like rain on arid ground. All I needed or would ever need to live the normal Christian life was already mine in the person of the indwelling Christ and His indwelling Spirit.*[182]

Clothe Yourself in the Whole Armor of God

> *"Nothing fills demons with more fear than the name and the blood of Jesus. If a person dealing with demonically oppressed people fails to use the protection that God has provided for him, he will achieve nothing."*[183]

The believer must become proficient in the use of the mighty weapons and armor God has given to those who love Him and have received Jesus Christ

149

as Savior.

A chilling story comes from the events of "D Day" in World War II, as recorded by S. L. A. Marshall in his book Men Against Fire.

> *Only five infantry companies (on Omaha Beachhead, June 6,*
> *1944) were tactically effective. In these companies one-fifth of the*
> *men fired their weapons during the day-long advance from the*
> *water's edge   to the first row of villages - a total of not more*
> *than 450 men firing consistently...The best showing that could be*
> *made by the most spirited and aggressive companies was that one*
> *man in four had made some use of his fire power.[184]*

What would a survey of the church of Jesus Christ reveal about the soldiers of the cross and the use of their "fire power?" How many in the church are using the "weapons mighty through God" to advance on the enemy's strongholds and take down the gates of hell? R. Arthur Mathews has said,

> *Weapons do give an impressiveness to the soldier on the parade*
> *ground. But as soldiers facing an implacable foe, we have to realize*
> *that battles are won only by the soldier who fights, and fighting*
> *involves using a weapon. Unused weapons do not inflict casualties*
> *on the enemy or win wars.[185]*

The child of God who intends to live a victorious overcoming life will ever be in conflict with the enemy of God. Dr. Neal Anderson describes the dilemma.

> *Through these years of learning and ministering I have come to*
> *understand that there are two concepts which determine the victory*

and fruitfulness of a Christian. The first concept is maturity... God has given us everything we need to grow to maturity in Christ (2 Peter 1:3). But Satan is opposed to our maturity and will do anything he can to keep us from realizing who we are and what we have in Christ. Since we wrestle against principalities and power instead of flesh and blood (Ephesians 6:12), we must experience victory over the dark side before we can fully mature.[186]

The Apostle Paul gave regarding the enemy's effort to snare the believer and to build strongholds in their life (2 Corinthians 10:4-5; Ephesians 4:26-27; 2 Timothy 2:24-226). Believers "wrestle... against principalities, against powers, against the rulers of the darkness of this world, against spiritual wickedness in high [heavenly] places" (Ephesians 6:12).

In the word, 'wrestle,' (pale), Paul uses a Greek athletic term. Thayer defines as follows: 'a contest between two in which each endeavors to throw the other, and which is decided when the victor is able to press and hold down his prostrate antagonist, namely, hold him down with his hand upon his neck.' When we consider that the loser in a Greek wrestling contest had his eyes gouged out with resulting blindness for the rest of his days, we can form some conception of the Ephesian Greek's reaction to Paul's illustration. Christian wrestling against the powers of darkness is no less desperate and fateful.[187]

"Therefore," he said, "take up the full armor of God that you may be able to resist in the evil day, and having done everything, to stand firm."[188] The child of God is to do everything they can to resist the forces of darkness and to stand victoriously against the onslaught of the enemy's attack. God has made available a full complement of spiritual armor that makes victory possible.

> *For this conflict with the powers of darkness the believer must learn experimentally how to take and use the armour for the battle, described by the apostle in Ephesians vi. The objective in Ephesians vi. is clearly not victory over sin - this is assumed - but* **victory over Satan.** *The call is not to the world, but to the church. A call to stand in armour; to stand in the evil day; to stand against the powers of darkness; to stand after accomplishing the work of overthrowing them - "having overcome all," verse 13, a.v.m.- by the strength given of God.[189] [author's emphasis]*

Each piece of the believer's armor provides specific protection and weaponry against the forces of hell; enabling the righteous warrior to "stand firm" (Ephesians 6:14). "Many commentators and preachers affirm that all the weapons listed in Ephesians 6:14-17, with the possible exception of the sword of the Spirit, are defensive. A warrior who never attacks the enemy but only defends himself is a trapped warrior. An army that only defends but never attacks is unfit for war. A church which does not reach out to war but only stands and defends itself is already defeated."[190]

Six pieces of armor are listed in Ephesians 6:14-17. The belt of truth is to gird the believer, a breastplate of righteousness is to cover the torso, shoes of the preparation of the gospel of peace are to be worn, a shield of faith is to be carried, a helmet of salvation is to be worn upon the head, the sword of the Spirit, and the Word of God is to be in the hand, and prayer in the Holy Spirit is to be continually spoken. Proficient use of each weapon is significant for the effective and victorious warrior who intends to "withstand in the evil day and having done all to stand" (Ephesians 6:13).

The belt of truth is that piece of armor which was "especially used in keeping other parts in place, and in securing the proper soldierly attitude and freedom of movement."[191] "Stand therefore, having your loins girt about with truth," is in the middle voice of Greek grammar and not passive, as in the King James Version. Putting on the belt then is the personal responsibility of the believer. The truth that secures the believer's armor and gives him the freedom of movement is both the truth of the gospel of Jesus Christ, that is the Word of God, and the truthfulness of his own heart and word.

> *It is simplest and most accordant with usage to take it so here (in the sense of candor, sincerity, truthfulness), And this plain grace of openness, truthfulness, reality, the mind that will practice no deceits and attempt no disguises in our intercourse with God, is indeed vital to Christian safety and essential to the due operation of all other qualities of character* [192]

It is also the responsibility of the soldier of God to clothe himself with the breastplate of righteousness. This phrase also is in the middle voice. Kenneth Wuest describes this righteousness, which protects the heart from the death blows of the enemy, as a sanctifying righteousness rather than the righteousness which is imparted by God through justification. The breastplate of righteousness is confident identification of the believer with Jesus Christ and His finished work which has justified and removed all condemnation and accusation of the believer's sinful behavior. The Holy Spirit then gives the believer power to stand victorious in that righteousness and resist the wily temptations of the enemy and the passionate cravings of the flesh (Romans 8:12-14).

The third piece of armor is also stated in the Greek middle voice. The believer is to dress himself with the shoes of the preparation of "the Gospel of peace." Many commentators take the position that this passage is about evangelism, while others reference it strictly with the idea of spiritual warfare. It is difficult, grammatically, to establish this passage strictly upon one or the other position. I believe it is because both positions should be taken.

The soldier wore a special type of sandal as part of his armor.

> *The sandals, or shoes, which were probably made so as to cover the foot, and which often were fitted with nails, or armed with spikes, to make them hold firm in the ground: or with "greaves" that were fitted to the legs, and designed to defend them from any danger. These "greaves" or boots (1 Samuel 17:6) were made of brass, and were in almost universal use among the Greeks and Romans.* [193]

The foot, thus secure with the shoe and the shoe secure upon the turf, would allow the soldier to both stand firm in battle and move swiftly when advancing.

The warfare of the believer is both to protect himself from the attack of the enemy and to advance the kingdom of God. The feet of the righteous one should be secure and stable in its resistance to the forces of darkness, but also should be beautiful in carrying the Good News to heart of those who have not heard (Isaiah 52:7; Romans 10:15).

"Above all, taking the shield of faith." (Ephesians 6:16)

Lincoln states that Paul here uses thureos or scutum, for shield. It
is the 'large shield, four feet in length and two and half feet in width,
which is described by Polybius 6.23.2 as the first part of the
Roman panoplia and which protected the whole body."[194]

The believer's "large shield" of faith is their absolute trust, total confidence, and complete reliance upon their position "in Christ."

The flaming missiles of the evil one" (NAS) is analogous of the fiery arrows used in ancient warfare. The tips were covered with tar and set on fire. The powers of darkness will shoot flaming missiles of immoral behavior, unloving conduct, false teaching, persecution, doubt and despair against the mind and heart of the believer.

The child of God must learn to trust who they are *in* Christ. They must confidently know they are seated with Christ in heavenly places; clothed with His righteousness; free from all condemnation; and unshakable in the love of Christ. With that confident faith they will be able to extinguish every flaming missile the enemy sends their way.

The helmet of salvation is protection from the most fatal blows the enemy can deliver. The apostle exhorts the believer to *take* the helmet. "The one verb 'take' applies to both pieces of armor listed next. 'The verb has its proper sense here, not merely 'take' but 'receive,' i.e., as a gift from the Lord, a thing provided and offered by Him.'"[195] The helmet of salvation, which the believer receives as a gift from the Lord Jesus Christ, is justification and eternal life through faith in Jesus Christ's completed work.

When the enemy would crush the head of the believer with accusations and condemnation or thoughts of despair and defeat, they are fully protected and able to resist the attack of darkness "by the blood of the Lamb and by the word of their testimony" (Revelation 12:11).

The sixth mighty weapon every believer must have in their arsenal is the "sword of the Spirit." The Greek word used is *machaira*, describing the shorter sword used in close combat, as opposed to the *pouphaia*, or long sword. The short sword is a vital weapon for the godly soldier to parry the thrusts of the enemy and to deliver powerful offensive blows, as was exemplified by our Lord in His battle with Satan in the wilderness of Judea.

The sword is not mighty by human dynamic or charisma. It is the sword *of the Spirit*. Holy Spirit is the one who empowers the believer to stand strong and to wield the sword victoriously against the enemy. The prophet Isaiah said,

> *So shall they fear the name of the LORD from the west, and His glory from the rising of the sun. When the enemy shall come in like a flood, the Spirit of the LORD shall lift up a standard against him.*[196]

Adam Clarke gives the following commentary on the prophet's words.

> *Kimchi says, he that was the standard-bearer always began the battle by first smiting at the enemy. Here then, the Spirit of the Lord is the standard-bearer, and strikes the first blow. They who go against sin and Satan with the Holy Spirit at their head, are sure to win the day.*[197]

The sword which the believer is to brandish, in the power of the Holy Spirit, is the Word of God.

> *For the word of God is quick, and powerful, and sharper than any two-edged sword, piercing even to the dividing asunder of soul and spirit, and of the joints and marrow, and is a discerner of the thoughts and intents of the heart. Neither is there any creature that is not manifest in His sight: but all things are naked and opened unto the eyes of Him with whom we have to do.[198]*

Jesus used the Word of God to parry every thrust Satan made against Him in the wilderness temptation. When Satan said, "If you are the Son of God, command that these stones become bread;" Jesus said, "It is written, 'Man shall not live by bread alone, but on every word that proceeds out of the mouth of God'" (Matthew 4:3-4 NAS). When Satan said, "If you are the Son of God, throw yourself down for it is written, 'He will give His angels charge concerning you.' And 'On their hand, they will bear you up, lest you strike your foot against a stone;' Jesus answered, "On the other hand, it is written, 'You shall not put the Lord your God to a test'" (Matthew 4:6-7 NAS). When Satan showed Jesus "all the kingdoms of the world and their glory" and said to Him, "All these things I will give to you, if you fall down and worship me;" Jesus said to him, "Be gone, Satan! For it is written," 'You shall worship the Lord your God and serve Him only'" (Matt. 4:8-10 NAS).

With those last words from Jesus' mouth, the devil had to leave. Every believer has that same authority and power when they use the sword of the Spirit.

The last weapon placed at the disposal of every believer is prayer in the Holy Spirit. While some commentators choose not to regard prayer as a weapon (i.e. Dr. Ed Murphy), the scripture is replete with men and women using prayer as a mighty weapon against the enemy.

Moses interceded for Joshua and the Israeli army in Exodus 17:8-16. Esther, through Mordecai, called the Jews to fasting and prayer against the genocide established by Haman (Esther 4:13-17). King Hezekiah was only able to defeat the Assyrian army and Sennacherib through prayer (2 Chronicles 32:1-22). In Isaiah 58:6, he declared fasting and prayer as the weapon that releases the captive and breaks the yoke of bondage. Jesus said there were certain demonic forces that could only be defeated through fasting and prayer (Matthew 17:21).

Paul, the Apostle, included prayer when he was listing the armor of the soldier of God. He said the kind of prayer that will release captives, break off yokes and destroy enemy armies must have three characteristics. It must be motivated, directed, and empowered by the Holy Spirit. "With all prayer and supplication in the Holy Spirit," wrote the Apostle. It must be vigilant. "Watching there unto," is the instruction. "Watching is *agrupneo*, 'to be sleepless, keep awake.' It means 'to be attentive, vigilant.' It is the opposite of listlessness, expressing alertness."[199] It must be given constant attention, 'with all perseverance." Perseverance is the Greek word *proskartereo*, meaning "to give unremitting care to a thing."[200] The child of God must give unremitting attention to prayer in the Holy Spirit.

This kind of Holy Spirit praying will bring great exploits for the kingdom of God and do serious damage to the strongholds of darkness, as will be seen in the next chapter.

Clothed with Power from on High

Jesus spent forty days after His resurrection giving final instructions to His followers. He clearly established the mission of the church and commanded them to go into all the world and make other disciples (Matthew 28:19). During His last meeting with them He gave strict orders they were not to attempt any of the work He had assigned until they had been "clothed with power from on high." Luke records these instructions.

> *And he said unto them, These are the words which I spake unto you, while I was yet with you, that all things must be fulfilled, which were written in the law of Moses, and in the prophets, and in the psalms, concerning Me. Then opened He their understanding, that they might understand the scriptures. And said unto them, Thus it is written, and thus it behooved Christ to suffer, and to rise from the dead the third day: And that repentance and remission of sins should be preached in His name among all nations, beginning at Jerusalem. And ye are witnesses of these things. And, behold, I send the promise of my Father upon you: but tarry ye in the city of Jerusalem, until ye be endued with power from on high. And He led them out as far as to Bethany, and He lifted up His hands, and blessed them. And it came to pass, while He blessed them, He was parted from them, and carried up into heaven.*[201]

Why would Jesus give such orders? He had trained the men and women for three years. They had been on successful missions previously. What was the importance of these orders to "wait?" The writer, Luke, clarified in his second book to Theophilus.

> *And, being assembled together with them, commanded them that they should not depart from Jerusalem, but wait for the promise of the Father, which, saith He, ye have heard of Me. For John truly baptized with water; but ye shall be baptized with the Holy Ghost not many days hence.*

> *But ye shall receive power, after that the Holy Ghost is come upon you: and ye shall be witnesses unto Me both in Jerusalem, and in all Judaea, and in Samaria, and unto the uttermost part of the earth.*[202]

The importance of "waiting" was to be found in the gift the followers would receive ten days later. Heavenly Father was going to send the gift of the baptism of the Holy Spirit to the church, in fulfillment of the prophecy of Joel 2:28. Holy Spirit baptism would bring the necessary power to fulfill the Great Commission.

Living the Spirit-empowered life is critical to victorious Christian living. Without Holy Spirit power nothing can be accomplished of lasting benefit. He is one who enables the child of God to live victorious over the passions of the flesh (Galatians 5:16). He is the source of Christ-like character (Galatians 55:22-23). He will renew the mind (Ephesians 2:22; Romans 12:2). He brings spiritual edification (1 Corinthians 14:1-4; Jude 20-21). He is the inspiration and guide for prayer (Romans 8:26-27). He is the power for witnessing (Acts. 1:8). He is the giver of spiritual gifts (1 Corinthians 12:1-11). He is the one who makes the preached word have life (2 Corinthians 3:3-6). He is the one who confirms the Word of God with power (1 Corinthians 2:4-

5).

The soldier of God who has been born again of the Holy Spirit, equipped with the "whole armor of God;" firmly established in his unshakable position *in* Jesus Christ; and clothed with power from on high, is ready to do mighty exploits for the kingdom of God. They are fully capable of crashing the gates of hell and to establish the kingdom of God. They are equipped to plunder the enemy's camp to populate heaven.

The Power of Intercessory Prayer

My Dear Wormwood,

The real trouble about the set your patient is living in is that it is merely Christian. They all have individual interests, of course, but the bond remains mere Christianity. What we want, if men become Christians at all, is to keep them in the state of mind I call 'Christian'. And if they must be Christians, let them at least be Christians with a difference. Substitute for faith itself some Fashion.

Your Affectionate Uncle

Screwtape

Lewis, The Screwtape Letters

It was a terrible blight on the community. Captain Coyote's was one of the most popular bars in town, hosting strippers three nights a week. One night was for women to watch male strippers and two nights for men to watch women. The patrons would line up clear around the block waiting to get in each night.

During one of my days of prayer and fasting the Lord impressed upon me to begin making prayer drives around Captain Coyote's; praying for the place to close down and the building to become a gospel preaching church. Immediately, I began making prayer drives around the property. One day the Lord asked me drive around it seven times and to declare the strongholds to come down.

163

A few weeks after that word began to circulate Captain Coyote's was going to close. The owner was bankrupt and going out of business. I was amazed, but the story does not end there.

Several weeks later I received word that a new pastor had moved into town from Oregon. He had purchased the Captain Coyote's property and was starting a new church. That pastor became a friend and I was privileged to serve the first communion service held in the new church. The altar was located on the very location where the bar had been.

God's Promise to His Son and the Church

God has a passion to displace darkness and bring His light. The church of Jesus Christ has been given authority to displace devils from individual lives (Matthew 10:7-8; Mark 16:17; Acts 8:5-7; 19:11-12; 1 Corinthians 12:10); to bless homes with peace (Luke 10:5-7); and to drive back the kingdom of darkness from neighborhoods, cities and regional areas (Ezekiel 22:30-31; Matthew 10:11-15; Luke 10:8-15). God promised His Son and the church:

> *Ask of Me, and I will surely give the nations as Thine inheritance,*
> *And the very ends of the earth as Thy possession. Thou shalt break*
> *them with a rod of iron. Thou shalt shatter them like earthenware.*[203]

The church has been given the authority to bring the kingdom of God into situations, circumstances and even neighborhoods and cities. Jesus said, "When you pray say, 'Our Father which art in heaven, hollowed be Thy name, Thy kingdom come, Thy will be done on earth as it is in heaven'"

164

(Matthew 6:9-10). This is a significant part of the church taking the keys of the kingdom and crashing the gates of hell (Matthew 16:19-20). The Apostle Paul wrote to the church in Ephesus.

> *And to bring to light what is the administration of the mystery which for ages has been hidden in God, who created all things; in order that the manifold wisdom of God might now be made known through the church to the rulers and the authorities in the heavenly places. This was in accordance with the eternal purpose which He carried out in Christ Jesus our Lord.*[204]

Examples of this authority are given to us in the Scriptures. God responded with grace when Abraham interceded for Sodom and Gomorrah (Genesis 18:20-33). God had compassion when Hezekiah and Isaiah interceded for Jerusalem (2 Chronicles 32:1-22). An entire city in Samaria turned to Jesus Christ (Acts 8:5-25). The city of Ephesus was shaken to its very spiritual foundation under the ministry of the Apostle Paul (Acts 19:8-41).

Is God Still Transforming Cities?

It should be asked, "Are there any modern day examples of God answering prayer and entire cities being shaken?" The answer is, "Yes!" George Otis, Jr. and the Sentinel Group have been tracking transformation work around the world for over ten years. They have identified no less than twelve cities and regions that are truly experiencing the visitation of God's glory and transformation.

In the mid-1970's, the town of Almolonga [Guatemala] was typical of many

Mayan highland communities: idolatrous, inebriated and economically depressed. Burdened by fear and poverty, the people sought support in alcohol and a local idol named Maximon. Determined to fight back, a group of local intercessors got busy, crying out to God during evening prayer vigils.

As a consequence of their partnership with the Holy Spirit, Almolonga...Has become one of the most thoroughly transformed communities in the world. A full 90 percent of the town's citizens now consider themselves to be evangelical Christians...Churches are now the dominant feature of Almolonga's landscape...bought out several distressed taverns and turned them into churches. This happened over and over again...One new bar did open...but it only lasted a couple of months. The owner was converted...For 20 years the town's crime rate has declined steadily. In 1994, the last of Almolonga's four jails closed...Whereas before they would export four truckloads of produce per month, they are now watching as many as 40 loads a day roll out of the valley.

Nicked named 'America's Vegetable Garden,' Almolonga's produce is of biblical proportions...five-pound beets, carrots larger than [a man's arm], cabbages the size of oversized basketballs...[205]

God loves to transform cities and make them into declarations of His glory, when individuals and churches will partner with Him. Europe was transformed by the prayers and intercession of Martin Luther, John Huss, John Calvin and the Moravians. John Wesley and George Whitefield were used by God to bring transformation to England. Even slavery was broken by the intervention of leaders, like William Wilberforce, who had become

Christians.[206] America also experienced transformation through the intercession of men like Jonathan Edwards, Timothy Dwight and others.

A Park Transformed for God

"I want you to believe me to establish my righteousness there." The words came to my heart with such force there was no doubt the Lord was calling me to take up an intercession for the Mount Scott Park. It was a beautiful park, four city blocks long and two wide; wonderfully shaded by large pine trees; perfect for families with swings, park benches, picnic tables, tennis court and a ball field.

No families came to the park. Drug dealing and the dangers that go along with that traffic, kept them away. Two years went by as I went around that park three and four times a week praying for God's glory and righteousness to be established there. Little by little the stronghold began to break. After two years, drug traffic began to diminish and families began to come back. Today there is a new aquatic center built in the park. It is full of families all spring and summer.

Only by earnest prayer and intercession do these kinds of transformations take place. The church is to rescue souls out of the darkness and bring them into kingdom of God. Isaiah the prophet declared, "And I will give thee the treasures of darkness, and hidden riches of secret places, that thou mayest know that I, the

LORD, *which call thee by thy name, am the God of Israel"*
(Isaiah 45:3).

Believers Must Press the Kingdom

Believers must take up the call and press the kingdom of Satan with the authority of Jesus' name and the power of His blood. Then captives can be released; strongholds of darkness taken down and transformation happen in the lives of individuals and cities. It may be porn shops or drug houses; coworkers or unsaved family members; neighbors or friends, God is looking for those who will allow Him to show Himself mighty by rescuing souls and driving back darkness.

For our transgressions are multiplied before Thee, and our sins testify against us: for our transgressions are with us; and as for

our iniquities, we know them; In transgressing and lying against the LORD, and departing away from our God, speaking oppression and revolt, conceiving and uttering from the heart words of falsehood. And judgment is turned away backward, and justice standeth afar off: for truth is fallen in the street, and equity cannot enter. Yea, truth faileth; and he that departeth from evil maketh himself a prey: and the LORD saw it, and it displeased Him that there was no judgment. And He saw that there was no man, and wondered that there was no intercessor: therefore, His arm brought salvation unto him; and his righteousness, it sustained him.[207]

God has promised when the church will accept that responsibility that "…those from among you will rebuild the ancient ruins; you will raise up the age-old foundations; and you will be called the repairer of the breach, the restorer of the streets in which to dwell."[208]

What Qualities Are Necessary for Effectiveness?

How can the church have such effectiveness and power in intercession? The heart of the believer must become broken with that which breaks the heart of God. The individual or group of believers must be willing to spend quality time in prayer and waiting on God until His Holy Spirit purifies and brings their heart into alignment with Him (Isaiah 58:1-10). The believers must learn to pray in the Holy Spirit (Romans 8:26-27; Ephesians 6:18-19; Jude 20-21). The great intercessor, Reese Howells, learned this important lesson from the Holy Spirit.

> *Now the Spirit told him, 'the meaning of prayer is answer and of all that I give you, see that you lose nothing.' He also told him that effectual praying must be guided prayer, and that he was no longer to pray for all kinds of things at his own whim or fancy, but only the prayer that Holy Ghost gave him.*[209]

The believer must learn to exercise the authority of Jesus' name and the power of His blood over the lives of individuals and areas they want to free from the strongholds of Satan (Acts 4:23-31). The believer must allow the Holy Spirit to give them a prayer strategy. Study the neighborhoods; learn what are the strongholds and the spiritual history of the individual and area. *Informed Intercession*, by George Otis, Jr., is an excellent volume for learning this skill. The believer must persevere and not give up (Luke 11:1-13). The believer must stay humble and be ever learning the skills of prayer and intercession (Luke 11:1).

The Heart and Passion of God

Greed, violence, drunkenness and immorality were corrupting the very soul of the city. Bribes turned the head of judges and city officials. Justice was only available to those who had the influence and the finances to purchase it. The religious leaders were just as corrupt. God's heart grieved over the scene.

> *And the word of the LORD came to me saying, 'Son of man, say to her, 'You are a land that is not cleansed or rained on in the day of indignation. There is a conspiracy of her prophets in her midst, like a roaring lion tearing the prey. They have devoured lives; they have taken treasure and precious things; they have made many widows in the midst of her. Her priests have done violence to My law and have profaned My holy things; they have made no distinction between the holy and the profane, and they have not taught the difference between the unclean and the clean; and they hide their eyes from My sabbaths, and I am profaned among them. Her princes within her are like wolves tearing the prey, by shedding blood {and} destroying lives in order to get dishonest gain. And her prophets have smeared whitewash for them, seeing false visions and divining lies for them, saying, 'Thus says the Lord GOD,' when the LORD has not spoken. The people of the land have practiced oppression and committed robbery, and they have wronged the poor and needy and have oppressed the sojourner without justice.'* [210]

How would God deal with such corruption and injustice? He "searched for a man among them who should build up the wall and stand in the gap before Me for the land, that I should not destroy it; but I found no one. Thus I have poured out my indignation on them..."[211]

When the human race had become so corrupt "their thoughts were only evil continually," God looked for a man to intercede and preach to the people for one hundred and twenty years. He found Noah (Genesis 6:1-8; 2 Peter 2:5). When the men and women of Sodom and Gomorrah had filled their lives and their city with immorality, God looked for a man to intercede for them city and found Abraham (Genesis 18:20-33). When Israel turned to a golden calf idol and acted immorally Moses interceded for them (Exodus 32:7-14). When the king and residents of Nineveh became corrupt God found the prophet Jonah to go and preach repentance to city that they might be saved (Jonah 1-4).

God's heart and passion is not to bring judgment upon a city, but to find someone who will "build up the wall and stand in the gap" until the power of darkness is broken off the city and the people are saved.

God is looking someone who will have His heart and His passion for your city. Will you be that person?

Appendix 1

Can a Christian Have a Demon

Possibly the most controversial issue of spiritual warfare surrounds the question, "Can Christians be demon possessed?" It is an issue of great importance and must be dealt with scripturally. Correct understanding of the question surrounds two further questions that will guide our scriptural search: What does it mean to be a Christian? What is the difference between demon *possession* and being *demonized* or *to have a demon*?

Dr. Ed Murphy is known for his teaching on counseling and spiritual warfare. He serves as Vice President of Overseas Crusades and is Associate Professor of Bible and Missions at San Jose Christian College. He gives the following personal testimony.

> *Most Christians would categorically reject the possibility of the demonization of true believers. This was my position during most of my years in Christian ministry. In fact, most of us who have reversed our position on this matter were brought up with the traditional view of the non-demonization of believers. We changed primarily because of accumulated experience in counseling the demonized. This has led to renewed scriptural studies and a re-examination of the position of the post-apostolic church fathers on this subject.[212]*

A re-examination of the Scripture is called for and it is important.

What Does It Mean to Be a Christian?

Dr. Ed Murphy used an interesting term when he talked about the demonization of *true believers*. Most of the arguments heard over the years are reflected in a statement I made in the fall of 1982 when teaching on this very subject. *"Those supposed Christians who are demon possessed have not really been born again. If they had been, they could not possibly be demon possessed, because the Holy Spirit and a demon cannot dwell in the same body."* That is the position held by most Christian denominations and Bible colleges in the United States.

What is the scriptural requirement for a person to be a *true believer?* Jesus answered that question succinctly. "Except a man be born again he cannot enter the kingdom of God" (John 3:3). The following requirements are given in Scripture for a person to be born again. Confess with the mouth and believe in the heart that Jesus Christ is the Son of God, crucified on the cross and risen from the dead (Romans 10:9-10). Confess all sin and ask Jesus Christ for forgiveness (1 John 1:9). Receive Jesus Christ as Lord and Savior by faith (John 1:12; Ephesians 2:8-9).

When a person is truly born again are they no longer vulnerable to demons?

> *'I did notice that shortly after I arrived I began to tire mentally rather badly. This is attributed to the change in climate and weather conditions. Since I was convinced that Satan could not touch one of God's anointed, I thought little about it.' As the fatigue and*

depression increased, the missionary looked forward to a vacation. The vacation came and went without the slightest relief. He gradually convinced himself he was finished as a missionary and could not possibly return after his first furlough.

'I always maintained a high standard of fellowship with the Lord. There was not unconfessed sin in my life, and yet I was extremely unhappy, no joy in the Lord, bad nerves, the kind of depression medicine could not help'

At this point, [he] thought that evil spirits were influencing him but quickly dismissed the idea since his orthodox belief made it impossible. Whenever he attended church he felt even more depressed the next day. His temper raged out of control and it was nearly impossible to sleep at night. A major decision was reached -- give up Christianity completely. For him it was total failure.

At this point, the Holy Spirit intervened. One single thought that simply overpowered him, 'Why don't you fast and pray and cast them out?' In desperation he reached for the Bible...turned to Matthew and read.

'Howbeit this [kind] evil spirit goeth not out but by prayer and fasting.'

He decided to kneel and pray using the words, 'In the name of Jesus who shed His blood on Calvary for me, I command you, spirit of mental depression to depart from me and return no more.' His

175

depression began to lift, his confusion ceased, and his sense of failure
vanished as total deliverance came.[213]

What Does It Mean to Be Demonized?

Dr. Murphy says, "Not a single verse of Scripture states that the Holy Spirit cannot or will not dwell in a human body or any other area, where demons are present."[214] The Apostle Paul agrees. He states in his letter to the church at Ephesus. "Be ye angry, and sin not: let not the sun go down upon your wrath: Neither give place to the devil" (Ephesians 4:26-27). The context of this statement is calling believers to live "not as other Gentiles walk, in the vanity of their mind, having the understanding darkened, being alienated from the life of God through the ignorance that is in them, because of the blindness of their heart. But ye have not so learned Christ. That ye put off the old man. Be renewed in the spirit of your mind; And put on the new man." (Ephesians 4:17-24).

Give place to the devil means to give an area of jurisdiction to a demon. The Greek word for *place* is *topos* (Strong's number 5117).

> *1. prop. Any portion of space marked off, as it were, from*
> *surrounding space; used of a). An inhabited place, as a city, village*
> *of a house seat one gets at a gathering. 2. metaph. a) The condition*
> *or station held by one in any company or assembly b) Opportunity,*
> *power, occasion for acting the thing for which influence is sought.*[215]

A believer can give space in their heart and life to demonic spirits. When space is given the demon has influence, authority and powers in that area of the person's life. Other scriptures bear this out, as well.

> *A certain woman came to Christ completely bent forward. She was mastered for 18 years by a demon sickness, (Luke 13:11) and yet she was identified as a person of faith. And who identified her as a person of faith? It was Jesus Christ Himself.*

> *And ought not this woman, a daughter of Abraham who Satan has kept bound for 18 years, be loosed form this bond on the Sabbath day? (Luke 13:16) Some people believe that Jesus was simply identifying the woman as a Jewess. This was not necessary because he was addressing an audience of Jews. He was identifying her as a believer that had been bound by the power of Satan for 18 years and was about to be loosed by the powerful hand of Jesus Christ.[216]*

Confusion on this issue is compounded by misunderstanding the difference between being *possessed* by a devil and one being *demonized*. This can be clarified by knowing the different levels of demonic activity and understanding how they work (see Chapter 4). Oppression, suppression and obsession are progressively greater levels demonic influence.

Obsession is when the demon has gained a foothold and controls an area of the person's life. This is being *demonized* but not *possessed*. It does require deliverance through Jesus Christ for the person to gain freedom.

Possession is a matter of ownership, not just influence or area control.

Demon possession can never be in the life of a *true believer*. Jesus Christ is Lord and Savior of their life and He has ownership not a demon.

Appendix 2

Multiple Personality Disorder

(MPD)

'You know how you play games at home?' My teacher asks, her
eyebrows raised. Mrs. Brewster is very nice. She has short sandy-
colored hair and her hands are soft. 'How many of you play games
at home?'

Tommy sits next to me and he raises his hand. Kim sits next to me
and she raises her hand. I don't raise my hand.

'You can play checkers or Parcheesi.'

The teacher wants us to think about the last time we played a game
together with our family. I'm thinking of one of the games we play
in our house. My older brother and his friends play a game with me
and his gun. I can smell the gun as someone puts it up to the side of
my head. It smells smoky the way a gun smells after it shoots. I
think I can hear the sound of the trigger being squeezed. I can hear
my heart jumping. I blink when the click comes and look quickly to
see if I can still see. This time I'm not dead. Each boy takes a

turn. If the gun doesn't go off, he gets to take me as his wife. Then
it's the next boy's turn

'Aren't games fun?' The teacher smiles and asks.

I am thinking of another game my father and Rudy play with me.
Usually they drink a lot of beer first. Then they make a game of
trying to smother me. They put the square pillow from the couch
over my face and hold it there.

'What other games do you play at home?'

I mustn't tell. Never. Ever. Or I will get my 'reward' from my
father; the payment for telling. If I ever tell anyone about the hidden
things, the games we play at home, my father makes it very, very
clear what he will do to me. Don't tell or I'll peel your skin off with
a knife,' he hisses through his clinched teeth. He holds each of my
small arms tightly in his big hands and lifts me up off the ground as
he speaks. As I look into his fiery, squinting eyes, I know that he
will do as he promises.[217]

Child abuse is one of the sad realities of life that almost no one wants to
discuss and the church is notorious for ignoring and sweeping it under the
carpet. Child abuse has been part of the human race since mankind's fall into
sin.

Of the six major doors through which demons attach themselves to
the lives of human beings, the door of child abuse is perhaps the
most common, most hideous, and the most destructive. It is

180

*universally agreed that child abuse, if terrible enough and if
continued over a long enough period of time, injures the child for the
rest of his life. Demons exploit this injury to their evil purposes.*[218]

The Consequences of MPD

The most hideous of child abuse is Satanic Ritualistic Abuse (SRA). SRA
leads to Multiple Personality Disorder (MPD) as well as demonization. MPD,
also referred to as *alter personalities*, is not the same as being demonized. One
may have a *multiple* that is not a demonic manifestation. On the other hand,
one who has MPD may also have demonic personalities. Dr. Murphy
explains.

> *Alter personalities and demons are not the same. Alters are
> fragmented parts of the host personality. Demons are alien
> personalities who seek to live within the body of human beings. They
> are not part of the host personality but spiritual invaders. Like
> dangerous germs and viruses, they enter where they do not belong."*[219]

The impact SRA has on a child and their personality is so severe and so long
lasting it is almost impossible to adequately describe. It is a weapon Satan is
using to gain control over children and to hold them captive for a life time.
When successful, he has at his disposal a human life for accomplishing his
evil plans.

> *The worst possible type of abuse occurring today is Satanic Ritual
> Abuse (SRA), a combination of all four forms of abuse. It is*

religious abuse performed on a child to cause unspeakable pain. It is physical abuse relation to sexual abuse, often rape and perversion of every imaginable and unimaginable type. It results in the most extreme form of psychological damage. The growing child is preprogrammed through this ultimate evil to malfunction as a youth and as an adult. Often the abuse splits the personality of the child, producing personality disassociation leading to Multiple Personality Disorder (MPD). Research reveals that 75 percent or more of MPDs resulted from SRA and related forms of extreme child sexual abuse...

In SRA the abuse is carefully calculated to produce enough trauma, torture, and pain so the child will dissociate. The abuse is continued until the dissociation is well established. Demons are conjured up or down to attach themselves to these personality segments. They are programmed (for lack of a better word) to gain control of the host person later in life for Satan and evil.[220]

Ministry to the Victims

It is critically important to understand the distinction between mental illness and demonization. There are mental disorders that are not demon related. They extend from other issues such as physical illness, chemical imbalance, birth defect or relationship issues.

I fully agree with Dr. Murphy when he says, "Every serious multiple I have dealt with has had demonic problems associated with his multiplicity."[221] But, not every *alter* is a demonic manifestation. The goal of the counseling and

182

ministry must be to reunite the fragmented personality of the individual through bringing each personality to saving grace in Jesus Christ.

The following are important ministry insights shared by Dr. Murphy from the writings of Reverend Earnest Rockstad, an early pioneer in recognizing and ministering to those with MPD.

"In our counseling - we are dealing with Christians - we have the person declare, 'I renounce Satan. I confess Jesus Christ as my Lord.' Then I make an affirmation and pray. 'I declare that we refuse to have in this time anything but the work of God.' Then I begin to command, 'In the name of the Lord Jesus I call for the John Doe' here who has not renounced Satan and has not accepted Jesus Christ as Lord. Is there a 'John Doe" here who does not know the Lord Jesus? Will you come to attention?' When you call for the segment to come, the change can be immediate or it may be gradual, a grin comes on the face - you can tell that somebody else is there. But sometimes it comes gradually, and I have been fooled on this. I keep checking. 'Do you confess Jesus Christ as Lord?' And when it is a character which has come up it will be very perplexed. 'Well, I don't know. I don't know what you are talking about.' The difference between a personality segment and a demon is that a demon will never renounce Satan. But when you explain to this segment [alter] about Satan. [They] Immediately say, 'Well I sure don't want anything to do with him.' And when you present the truth about Christ eventually there is a willingness to submit.'[222]

Every MPD case requires great love; enduring patience; wisdom from the

Holy Spirit; and very large amounts of time. It is a lengthy journey to bring the person to healing. It may take years.

Laura concludes her book with these beautiful words.

> *The healing that the Lord has done in my life can only be called dramatic. Both emotionally and spiritually, He has put the pieces back together and rebuilt what was destroyed.*[223]

Appendix 3

Dealing with Jezebel

Word arrived from the Queen. "I will kill you for what you did!" The prophet knew very well this was no casual threat; for Queen Jezebel had killed many of God's servants (1 Kings 18:4). Emotionally weary and physically exhausted, waves of discouragement began to sweep over him. "OK, Lord, I have had enough. Take my life; I am no better than my ancestors." The prophet of God was under major spiritual attack (1 Kings 19:1-10).

Elijah had done serious damage to the kingdom of darkness. The nation of Israel had been in a draught for three and a half years because they had turned their hearts from worshipping the true God to idolatry. Elijah challenged the prophets of Baal to a contest. They would build an altar and make a sacrifice to their god. The one who answered by sending fire to consume the sacrifice would be the true living God.

The prophets of Baal cut themselves and begged their god to answer. Baal was a lifeless and anemic idol, with no ears to hear or power to send fire. Jehovah, the God of Abraham, Isaac and Jacob, He answered by sending fire from heaven that consumed the altar and the sacrifice. He alone is the Almighty God of heaven and earth. Israel repented for worshipping false gods and the prophets of Baal were executed. Elijah prayed and rain was restored to the Land of Israel (1 Kings 18:20-40). The response of hell was swift.

Satan's chief ambassador and prophetess of Baal, responded immediately, sending a death threat to the prophet of the Living God. Feeling isolated and vulnerable, he fled to Mount Horeb. Elijah met God on the mountain with a fresh word that lifted his faith, brought new courage, and sent him on an assignment (1 Kings 19:1-13).

God assured His prophet he was not alone. Seven thousand men of God still lived in Israel who had not compromised and bowed the knee to Baal. Elijah was sent to the Valley of Abelmeholah to anoint the man who would succeed Elijah as the prophet of God.

A Solemn Warning to the Church

Elijah is not the only minister of God to be challenged and intimidated by Jezebel. Jesus Christ warned the church about the dangers of the spirit of Jezebel.

And unto the angel of the church in Thyatira write; these things saith the Son of God, who hath His eyes like unto a flame of fire, and His feet are like fine brass; I know thy works, and charity, and service, and faith, and thy patience, and thy works; and the last to be more than the first. Notwithstanding I have a few things against thee, because thou sufferest that woman Jezebel, which calleth herself a prophetess, to teach and to seduce my servants to commit fornication, and to eat things sacrificed unto idols. And I gave her space to repent of her fornication; and she repented not.[224]

The church at Thyatira had some very fine qualities that every pastor would hope for the church he pastors. They were known for their love, service and faith. They were people who had patience in working with people. But, they were also known by the Lord Jesus Christ to be a congregation that tolerated the same thing Ahab, King of Israel had tolerated. They allowed the spirit of Jezebel to be in their midst. The same spirit that motivated and animated the queen of Israel and persecuted the prophets of the living God was allowed to operate in the church of the living God.

Jesus gave a solemn warning with a promise of hope. "I gave her time to repent; and she does not want to repent."

> *But unto you I say, and unto the rest in Thyatira, as many as have*
> *not this doctrine, and which have not known the depths of Satan, as*
> *they speak; I will put upon you none other burden. But that which*
> *ye have already hold fast till I come. And he that overcometh, and*
> *keepeth my works unto the end, to him will I give power over the*
> *nations: And he shall rule them with a rod of iron; as the vessels of*
> *a potter shall they be broken to shivers: even as I received of my*
> *Father. And I will give him the morning star. He that hath an ear,*
> *let him hear what the Spirit saith unto the churches.*[225]

The Characteristics of a Jezebel Spirit

Brown-Driver-Briggs Dictionary and Lexicon defines Jezebel as "Baal exalts, Baal is husband to, unchaste."[226] Gesenius gives more insight. He says, means "without cohabitation, chaste, modest, a very suitable female name, not to be estimated from the conduct of the celebrated Jezebel of Tyre."[227]

Jezebel is not what she appears and will only abide in relationships she can control and dominate. She will appear to have a servant's heart and a humble spirit, but does so only to gain an advantage and to manipulate for she will yield to no one. It is very important to note these characteristics.[228] This spirit is attracted to female personalities and bodies. This spirit targets women who are bitter against men, insecure, jealous, vain, and desire to control others. It is fiercely independent. It is ambitious for position and control. It hates men and especially male authority. It is the source of obsession with sensuality. It brings a flood of witchcraft. It is the sprit behind women who publicly humiliate their husbands their tongue and then dominate and control him through fear of further humiliation. It uses sexual passions and perversions to control men. Sex is not the object or the goal. Control is the objective and aim. Physical contact is not necessary; the seductive look of the eye will capture the man.

A Jezebel spirit can only abide where there is an Ahab spirit; a man who will tolerate anything to gain what he wants. An Ahab spirit is filled with pride and will compromise to avoid trouble or confrontation. It will tolerate evil which allows men and women with dishonorable ambition of selfish and greedy agendas to gain position.

These characteristics are clearly scene in the lives of the historical couple who served as king and queen over Israel. Ahab was the son of Omri, King of Israel and became king following his father's death. "And Ahab, the son of Omri, did evil in the sight of the Lord above all that were before him" (1 Kings 16:30 KJV). He chose Jezebel, the daughter of Ethbaal the King of the Zidonians to be his wife. They choose to worship Baal and make him their

188

god. "Ahab did more to provoke the Lord God of Israel to anger than all the kings of Israel that were before him" (1 Kings 16:31-34).

Ahab was dominated by his wife and refused to stand up to her. He told Jezebel about Elijah and the execution of the prophets of Baal and refused to stop her threats against the prophet of God; even though he knew it was the living God that had consumed the altar of sacrifice and returned rain to Israel (1 Kings 19:1-2).

A man of Israel named Naboth, who lived in the Valley of Jezreel, own a very good vineyard. King Ahab wanted to buy the field. Naboth explained the vineyard had been a family inheritance and would not sell. The king behaved as a child throwing a temper tantrum, throwing himself upon his bed and refusing to eat. Jezebel comforted her little boy, "Don't cry for you are the king of Israel. Come and eat, I will get the vineyard for you" (1 Kings 21:1-7).

Such childish behavior and male weakness is the seed bed for the Jezebel spirit to grow and flourish. Ahab's wife secured the vineyard for him with a most cunning and evil plan, including the murder of Naboth. When she had received word that her plan had been executed she gave word to the king. "Arise, take possession of the vineyard of Naboth the Jezreelite, which he refused to give thee for money: for Naboth is not alive, but dead" (1 Kings 21:8-16). Apparently, Ahab asked no questions as to the sudden death of Naboth. He simply seized possession of the new toy he had wanted.

The Works of a Jezebel Spirit

Jesus warned the church at Thyatira of the evil work the spirit of Jezebel will plan and execute in the church, if left unchecked. She will seek to find her place among people who have love, faith, service and perseverance; especially those who are seeking to be deeply dedicated (Revelation 2:19). She has an unnatural attraction to people, especially to men in authority. The pulpit is her goal (1 Kings 21:25; 2 Kings 9:30-32; Revelation 2:20). She will seek out information and spread horrible stories and half-truths to gain favor with other women and to take down authority (1 King 19:1-2; 2 Kings 9:8-16). She will use sensuality to gain control (2 Kings 9:30-32). She will use prophetic words and the role of a teacher, as one who disciples others, to gain favor and control. She will have a reputation as one who is spiritually mature and strong in the Lord; claiming to have insights to truths and understanding others do not have (Revelation 2:20). She will seek out the hurting, insecure, fearful, wounded, weak and needy women to make them her disciples through leading them to new birth or bringing them under her authority as teacher and prophetess. She will seek to make "soul ties" with these women; dominate them and bring them to herself away from Godly and truthful leaders.

How Should a Jezebel Spirit Be Confronted?

Jesus commended those members in the church at Thyatira who "have not this doctrine and which have not known the depths of Satan, as they speak. I will put upon you none other burden" (Revelation 2:24).

The spirit of Jezebel must not be allowed to flourish in a church. The pastor and leaders must take purposeful and intentional steps to correct and remove the spirit from their midst. The leaders should study the life and works of Jehu (1 Kings 19:15-17; 2 Kings 9:1-37). God gave him the authority to deal with Jezebel by imparting a "commanding anointing." People may call those who operate in this anointing "mad." When the "commanding anointing" and the Word of God to deal with the Jezebel spirit in the church are honored, the people will see Jesus and reverence Him as King.

When the Jezebel spirit realizes the leader is going to deal with her and senses the leader has the anointing to drive her out she will seek peace (2 Kings 9:17-21; Revelation 2:21). She will give the appearance of peace but not seek genuine repentance. She speaks, "Peace" to the leaders and the congregation, but her actions are manipulative and subversive. You cannot make peace with Jezebel. The Lord Jesus will give her time to repent but she will not genuinely repent. There must be no giving into peace with Jezebel, no matter how much pressure will come from the congregation. Jezebel will manipulate the people by convincing them she has repented and is seeking peace. The people will believe her and put pressure on and threaten the leaders to make peace with the one operating by the spirit of Jezebel. Leaders are to be peacemakers but not with evil spirits, for we must not "give place to the devil" (Ephesians 4:27).

The Jezebel spirit is an evil spirit sent from the enemy to corrupt the church with idolatry and immorality (Revelation 2:20). The people around her and the Jezebel spirit, herself, will seek to make peace more than once. They will beg, scream and even plead for making peace. Leaders must *be alert* to the manipulation of the Jezebel spirit, as she will "make herself up" special for the leader in an effort to make peace (2 Kings 9:30). When Jezebel knows the leaders have received the anointing and been given the authority of the Word of God to deal with her, she will begin putting on makeup and dressing herself in a different outfit to appear acceptable. It is her effort to manipulate and take a different form and appearance but her spirit and her work has not changed. It is an effort to manipulate and pressure the "commanding

191

anointing" to back off and make room for her to remain. While the Jezebel spirit dresses to look differently and to make peace, she will be throwing condemnation at the leaders.

Jehu "drove furiously" to deal with Jezebel. Church leaders must cast down the Jezebel spirit in the congregation and all of its evil ways "furiously" (2 Kings 9:20). Jehu killed the sons of Ahab using his full strength. The church leaders must use the full power and strength of the Holy Spirit to deal with evil in their own lives and when driving out the Jezebel spirit and her evil in all of its forms and personalities; her children and her disciples committed to her spirit (2 Kings 9:24).

It was those who had been made eunuchs by Jezebel who teamed with Jehu and cast Jezebel out (2 Kings 9:32-33). Leaders should search for those in the congregation who have been made spiritually barren by the spirit of Jezebel and know her true spirit. The leaders should appeal to those who have been made barren to assist them in dealing with the Jezebel spirit and cast her out.

Jezebel was dealt with fully and completely by Jehu so she could not possibly remain alive (2 Kings 9:33). He trampled her body under the hooves of his horse. The Jezebel spirit must be totally destroyed out of the church and not allowed to remain in any measure or any form. The leaders may appear harsh and unmerciful at the level and strength in which they deal with the evil spirit. They must not back down or be intimidated by the people's cries for mercy. Jezebel must be totally destroyed and driven out of the church. Jehu should have no sorrow or grief for the death and destruction of Jezebel. There must be no sorrowing or grieving on the part of the leaders for casting out the Jezebel spirit. Just as no memorial was placed for Queen Jezebel, so no honor or memorial should be established for those who operate in the Jezebel spirit.

What Are the End Results for Jezebel and Her Disciples?

Jesus spoke specific words of judgment and destruction upon those who are animated by the spirit of Jezebel (Revelation 2:20-23). God will throw her into a "bed" of suffering. Those who are involved with her and embrace the spirit of Jezebel will go into the bed of destruction with her unless they repent and turn from their evil ways and renounce the evil spirit. Her children, those who are her disciples and her biological children will be struck dead. It not uncommon to see the biological children and grandchildren of a person operating under a Jezebel spirit to be spiritually lost and have no hunger, even great resentment for the things of Christ and the church. It common for her disciples to live in secret sins and have "a form of godliness but deny the power thereof" (2 Timothy 3:5).

Selected Bibliography

Anderson, Neil T. and Charles Mylander

    Setting Your Church Free Ventura: Regal Books 1994

    The Bondage Breaker Eugene: Harvest House Publishers. 1990

    Victory Over the Darkness Ventura: Regal Books 1990

Billheimer Paul E.

    Spiritual Warfare II Wheaton: Tyndale House Publishers 1982

Collins, Gary

    How to be A People Helper Santa Ana: Vision House 1976

    Search for Reality Wheaton: Key Publishers 1969

Colson, Charles and Nancy Pearcey

    How Now Shall We Live? Wheaton: Tyndale House Publishers 1999

Duewel, Wesley L.

    Mighty Prevailing Prayer Grand Rapids: Asbury Press 1990

Frangipane, Francis

    The Three Battle Grounds Advancing Church Publications 1989

Godwin, Rick

    Exposing Witchcraft in the Church Orlando Creation House 1997

Greene, Oliver B.

    Why Does the Devil Desire to Damn You? Greenville The Gospel Hour, Inc. 1966

Kock, Kurt

    Occult Bondage and Deliverance Kregel Publications 1981

    Between Christ and Satan Kregel Publications 1972.

LaHaye, Tim

You are Engaged in the Battle for the Mind Old Tappan Fleming H. Revell Company 1980.

Lewis. C. S.

The Screwtape Letters New York The McMillan Company 1961

Mathews, Arthur R.

Born for Battle, 31 Studies on Spiritual Warfare Robesonia: Overseas Missionary Fellowship, 1978

Muggeridege, Malcolm

Jesus, the Man Who Lives New York: Harper and Row Publishers, Inc. 1975

Murphy, Ed

The Handbook for Spiritual Warfare Nashville: Thomas Nelson1992

Otis, George, Jr.

The Last of the Giants Tarrytown: Fleming H. Revell 1991

Informed Intercession Ventura: Renew Books 1999

Twilight Labyrinth Grand Rapids: Chosen Books. 1997

Penn-Lewis, Jessie

War on the Saints New York: Thomas E. Lowe, Ltd. 1981

Silvoso, Ed

That None Should Perish Ventura: Regal Books 1994

Thieme, R.B. Jr.

Demonism 1974

Unger, Merrill F.

Biblical Demonology Wheaton: Scripture Press 1952

White, John Wesley

The Devil Wheaton: Tyndale House Publishers 1971

More Books from Dr. Hackett

The Freedom Series:

Discovering True Identity

Charis

The Disciples Series:

Discovering Jesus

The Joy of Becoming Like Jesus

Becoming Ambassadors for Christ

A Gift for You

Receive a free Bible reading plan and journal each month when you visit Foundational at fdeanhackett.com. At Foundational, we are passionate about getting families in Word of God and want to partner with you in building a strong foundation for future generations!

About Foundational

If you were inspired by Discovering True Identity and would like more information about how you can establish your identity in Jesus Christ, I encourage you to connect with Foundational. Foundational exists to help you build a strong foundation in your life and in the lives of your children so that we can raise up future generations that live passionately for Jesus Chirst.

To learn more about Foundational, you can contact us at dean@fdeanhackett.com, or visit fdeanhackett.com

ENDNOTES

i Merrill F. Unger, *Biblical Demonology* (Wheaton, Scripture Press Publications, 1956)

ii Josh McDowell and Don Stewart, *Handbook of Today's Theology* () 177-178

iii Malcolm Muggeridge, *Jesus, the Man Who Lives* (New York: Harper and Row Publishers, 1975) 51

iv Freda Lindsay, "World Prayer and Share Letter," Christ For The Nations Vol. 54, No. 4 (July 2001) 12

vWinston Churchill, *Great Destiny* (G.P. Putnam's Sons, 1965) 664-665

vi ibid. p. 667
7George Otis, Jr., *Twilight Labyrinth* (Grand Rapids, Chosen Books, 1997)

8 ibid

9 ibid. 149

[10] Jay A. Adams, *Competent to Counsel (Presbyterian and Reformed Publishing, 1974)*
[11] Psalm 51:5 NKJV
[12] Gary Collins, *Search for Reality* (Wheaton, Key Publishers, 1969) 22.-2
[13] 2 Corinthians 4:18 NKJV
[14] Hebrews 11:3 NKJV
[15] ibid. Otis, 13-14
[16] ibid. Murphy, 4
[17] ibid.
[18] ibid. Otis, 5
[19] ibid. Otis, 5
[20] 2 Kings 6:12 NKJV

[21] 2 Corinthians 2:9-11 NKJV

[22] Ephesians 6:10-13 KJV

[23] John 10:10 NKJV

[24] John Wesley White, *The Devil*, (Wheaton: Tyndale House Publishers, 1971) 107-108

[25] Job 1:6-11 NKJV

[26] Job 2:1-5 NKJV

[27] Proverbs 6:18 NKJV

[28] Colossians 1:13-14 NAS

[29] ibid. Otis, 13

[30] ibid

[31] Numbers 13:1-2 KJV

[32] Numbers 13:32-33 KJV

[33] op. cit. Funk and Wagnal

[34] James 1:13-16 KJV

[35] Psalms 51:5 NAS

[36] Romans 5:12-13 NAS

[37] Exodus 20:5-6 NAS

[38] Exodus 34:6-7 NAS

[39] Guy R. Lefrancois, *Of Children, An Introduction to Child Development* (Belmont: Wadsworth Publishing Company, 1973) 14

[40] op. cit., Adams 82 [footnote

[41] William J. Bennett, The Index of Leading Culture Indicators, (New York, Simon and Schuster, 1994)

[42] Psalms 139:13-16 KJV

[43] Ephesians 2:1-3 NAS

[44] I John 2:16 KJV

[45] 3 John 9-11 KJV

[46] Ezekiel 28:14-16 NAS

[47] Edward McNall Burns, *Western Civilizations, Eighth Edition* (New York: W.W. Norton & Company, Inc., 1873) 59-60

[48] John Foxe, *Foxe's Book of Martyrs* (Sprindale: Whitaker House, 1981) 12

[49] Kazimier Smolen, *Auschwitz 1940-1945*, Guide-Book Through the Museum (Katowice:

Krajowa Agencja Wydawnicza, 1981) 10-11

[50] 2 Cor. 10:4 KJV

[51] Psalms 60:12; 103:18 KJV

[52] Luke 4:18-19 NAS

[53] Exodus 1:8-13, 15-16 NKJV

[54] Exodus 6:6-8 NKJV

[55] Exodus 8:18-19 NAS

[56] Exodus 11:5 NAS

[57] Exodus 6:6 NAS

[58] John 1:29 NKJV

[59] Matthew 26:26-28 NKJV

[60] Matthew 2:2-8 NAS

[61] 1 John 3:8 KJV

[62] Colossians 1:15 KJV

[63] John 1:29 NKJV

[64] Matthew 4:1 KJV

[65] op.cit., Murphy 263

[66] Genesis 3:5 KJV

[67] Matthew 4:3; 5-6; 8-9 NAS

[68] Matthew 4:4, 7, 10 NAS

[69] op.cit., Murphy 268

[70] ibid

[71] op.cit. White 79-80

[72] Matthew 8:16 KJV

[73] Mark 3:11 NAS

[74] Revelation 12:10-11 NAS

[75] Matthew 3:3 NKJV

[76] Matthew 4:17 NKJV

[77] Matthew 4:23-25; 9:35 NKJV

[78] Matthew 12:22-25 NKJV

[79] Matthew 12:25-30 NKJV

[80] Acts 10:38 NKJV

[81] Luke 22:3-5 NAS

[82] John 13:26-27 NKJV

[83] Matthew 26:36-39, 42, 44 NAS

[84] Matthew 26:27-29 NKJV

[85] Isaiah 53:5-7 KJV

[86] Luke 22:48 NKJV

[87] Luke 22:66 NKJV

[88] Colossians 1:13-14 NAS

[89] Isaiah 59:2 NAS

[90] H.W.F. Gesenius, tran. Samule Prideaux Tragelles, *Gesenius' Hebrew and Chaldee Lexicon to the Old Testament Sriptures* (Grand Rapids: Baker Book Hous, 1979) 5780.

[91] R. Laird Harris, Gleason L. Archer, Jr., Bruce K. Waltke, *Theologcal Wordbook of the Old Testament* (Chicago: Moody Press, 1980) 650-651.

[92] The Online Bible thayer's Greek Lexicon and Brown Driver &Briggs Hebrew Lexicon, Copyright © 1993, Woodsid Bible Fellowship, Ontario, Canada. Licensed from the Institute for Creation Research

[93] Titus 2:14-15 KJV

[94] Matthew 26:59-60 KJV

[95] Leviticus 10:6 KJV

[96] Leviticus 21:10 KJV

[97] Luke 23:14-16 KJV

[98] Matthew 27:15-26 KJV

[99] Romans 3:10-18 KJV

[100] Revelation 20:11-15 KJV

[101] Romans 5:8-9 KJV

[102] op.cit., Thayer

[103] William Barclay, *The Daily Bible Study, The Letter to the Romans* (Philadelphia: The Westminster Press, 1957) 13-14

[104] Luke 23:13-17 NKJV

[105] Isaiah 53:3-5 KJV

[106] Op.cit.Gesenius

[107] Bill Gothard, *Men's Manual, Vol 1* (Oak Brook: Institute in Basic Youth Conflicts, 1979)

146-147

[108] ibid.

[109] Matthew 27:54 NAS

[110] Isaiah 53:5-6 NAS.

[111] 2 Corinthians 5:19-21 NIV

[112] Malcolm Muggeridge, *Jesus, the Man Who Lives* (New York: Harper and Row Publishers, Inc., 1975) 187.

[113] Guy P. Duffield, and Nathaniel M. Van Cleave, *Foundations of Pentecostal Theology* (Los Angeles: L.I.F.E. Bible College, 1983) 516

[114] David Sutton, *The Devil and His Demons* (A sermon delivered at Forty Fourth Avenue Baptist Church, Seattle, WA., November 6, 1994).

[115] Winston Churchill, <u>Great Destiny</u> (G.P. Putnam's Sons, 1965) 664-66

[116] Matthew 11:3-12 KJV

[117] Luke 16:16 NKJV

[118] Jack W. Hayford, *Spirit Filled Life Bible* (Nashville: Thomas Nelson Publishers, 1991)

[119] Matthew 10:16-22 NAS

[120] Edward Blaiklock, R.K. Harrison, David R. Douglass, *The New International Dictionary of Biblical Archaeology* (Grand Rapids: Zondervan Publishing, 1983) 112

[121] Matthew 16:17-19 NKJV

[122] 1 Corinthians 3:11 NKJV

[123] Luke 10:17 NKJV

[124] John 14:13-14 KJV

[125] Mark 16:15-17 KJV

[126] Acts 4:12 KJV

[127] Colossians 1:18 KJV

[128] Romans 8:31, 37 NKJV

[129] Luke 10:17 NAS

[130] Luke 10:18-19 NKJV

[131] Mark 16:15-16 NKJV

[132] Mark 16:17-18 NKJV

[133] Luke 4:18-19 NKJV

[134] op.cit. Churchill

[135] Ibid. P. 66

[136] op.cit. Ed Murphy, 341

[137] Matthew 17:5 KJV

[138] Matthew 17:19-20 NAS

[139] Acts 8:6-8 NAS

[140] 2 Corinthians 10:3-6 NAS

[141] op.cit. Unger, 101

[142] op.cit. Murphy, 348-349

[143] Acts 19:13-17 NAS

[144] Jude 9-10 NAS

[145]Ephesians 6:10-13 NKJV

[146] Matthew 16:19 KJV

[147] Earle E. Cairns, *Christianity Through the Centuries* (Grand Rapids: Zondervan Publishing House, 1954, 1981) 151

[148] Matthew 23:13 NAS

[149] Josh McDowell, Bob Hostetler, *Right from Wrong* (Dallas: Word Publishing, 1994) 251-266

[150] 1 Timothy 4:1 NKJV

[151] Rick Godwin, *Exposing Witchcraft in the Church* (Orlando: Creation House, 1997) 91

[152] Wesley L. Duewel, *Mighty Prevailing Prayer* (Grand Rapids: Asbury Press, 1990) 281-285

[154] Bill Subritzky, *Demons Defeated* (Aucklund: Dove Ministries, 1985) 18

[155] Psalms 149:5-9 NAS

[156] Psalm 8:1-2 NAS

[157] op.cit. Gesenius

[158] op.cit. Harris, Archer, Waltke

[159] op.cit. Duewel, 19

[160] Isaiah 58:6-12 NAS

[161] Revelation 12:7-12 KJV

[162] op.cit. Mathews, 37-38

[163] Neil T. Anderson, *Victory Over the Darkness* (Ventura: Regal Books, 1990) 12

[164] George Muller, ed. H. Lincoln Wayland, *Autobiography of George Muller, the Life of Trust* (Grand Rapids: Baker Book House, 1981 from the 1861 edition published by Gould and Lincoln (Boston) 77-78

[165] op.cit. Duewel, 92-93.

[166] Psalm 91:1-16 NAS

[167] John 8:36 NAS

[168] Romans 8:11-15 NKJV

[169] Watchman Nee, *The Spiritual Man* (New York: Christian Fellowship Publishers, 1968) Vol. II, 57

[170] The Online Bible Thayer's Greek Lexicon and Brown Driver & Briggs Hebrew Lexicon, Copyright (c)1993, Woodside Bible Fellowship, Ontario, Canada. Licensed from the Institute for Creation Research

[171] ibid

[172] op.cit. Wuest, 2 Peter, 22

[173] Deuteronomy 28:1-2 KJV

[174] Ephesians 1:3-7 KJV

[175] Neil T. Anderson, *The Bondage Breaker* (Eugene: Harvest House Publishers, 1990) 186

[176] op.cit., Watchman Nee, 13

[177] Romans 6:4-7 NAS

[178] Romans 6:4-5 NAS

[179] Romans 5:8-9 NAS

[180] Colossians 1:12-14 NAS

[181] Romans 8:31-39 NAS

[182] op.cit. Murphy, 7

[183] Kurt Koch, *Occult Bondage and Deliverance* (Grand Rapids: Kregel Publications, 1981) 109

[184] op.cit., Mathews, 55

[185] ibid., 54

[186] op.cit. Anderson, 11-12

[187] op.cit., Wuest, Ephesians, 143

[188] Ephesians 6:13 NAS

[189] op.cit., Penn-lewis, 253

[190] op.cit., Murphy, 408

[191] op.cit., Wuest, 143

[192] ibid.

[193] Barnes' Notes, Electronic Database. Copyright (c) 1997 by Biblesof

[194] op.cit., Murphy, 411

[195] ibid

[196] Isaiah 59:19 NAS

[197] Adam Clarke's Commentary, Electronic Database. Copyright (c) 1996 by Biblesof

[198] Hebrews 4:12-13 KJV

[199] op.cit. Wuest, 145

[200] ibid

[201] Luke 24:44-51 KJV

[202] Acts 1:4-5, 8 KJV

[203] Psalms 2:8-9 NAS

[204] Ephesians 3:9-11 NAS

[205] George Otis, Jr., *Informed Intercession* (Ventura: Renew Books, 1999) 18-22

[206] David A Fisher, *World History for Christian Schools* (Greenville: Bob Jones University Press, 1984) 473

[207] Isaiah 59:12-16 KJV

[208] Isaiah 58:12 NAS

[209] Norman Grubb, *Reese Howells, Intercessor* (Fort Washington: Christian Literature Crusade, 1984) 45

[210] Ezekiel 22:23-29 NAS

[211] Ezekiel 22:30-31 NAS

[212] op.cit., Murphy, 43

[213] David Sutton, *Can a Christian Be Demonized* (A Series of Teachings on Satan Taught at Forty Fourth Avenue Baptist Church) n.p

[214] op.cit., Murphy, 430

[215] Joseph Henry Thayer, trans., *Greek-English Lexicon of the New Testament, being Grimm's Wilke's Clavis Novi Testamenti* (Grand Rapids: Zondervan Publishing House, 1976)

[216] op.cit., Sutton

[217] Laura, *The Chained Lion*, A true Story by Laura (Colorado Springs: Lydia Press, 1999) 3-8

[218] op.cit., Murphy, 449

[219] ibid., 315

[220] idid., 439, 48

[221] ibid., 48

[222] ibid., 481-482

[223] op.cit., Laura, 234

[224] Revelation 2:18-21 KJV

[225] Revelation 2:24-29 KJV

[226] ibid

[227] Gesenius' Hebrew-Chaldee Lexicon of the Old Testamen

[228] I owe much of this material and research to Pastor Steve Stewart, Park Rose Assembly of God, Portland, Oregon and a message he delivered in August 2000

Made in the USA
Columbia, SC
21 December 2019

85617546R00126